A·LIFE·IN·TIME
AND·SPACE

A·LIFE·IN·TIME AND·SPACE

THE·BIOGRAPHY·OF·DAVID·TENNANT

NIGEL GOODALL

JOHN BLAKE

www.blake.co.uk

First published in hardback in 2008

ISBN: 978 1 84454 636 7

British Library Cataloguing-in-Publication Data:

A catalogue record for this book is available from the British Library.

Design by www.envydesign.co.uk

Printed in UK by CPI William Clowes, Beccles, NR34 7TL

1 3 5 7 9 10 8 6 4 2

Papers used by John Blake Publishing are natural, recyclable products made from
wood grown in sustainable forests. The manufacturing processes conform to the
environmental regulations of the country of origin.

Every attempt has been made to contact the relevant copyright-holders,
but some were unobtainable. We would be grateful if the appropriate
people could contact us.

Online praise for Nigel Goodall's previous books:

Kylie Naked (with Jenny Stanley-Clarke):
'To their credit, the authors don't try and shatter her girl-next-door image and her career is covered in almost bang up-to-date detail, including an extra chapter to take account of her recent success with 'Can't Get You Out Of My Head' and her fantastic performance at the 2002 Brit Awards. Hopefully the Princess of Pop will find time one day to pen her autobiography, but until then *Kylie Naked* is as thorough and enjoyable an account of her life as you could possibly want.'

Jonathan Weir, Amazon.co.uk

Winona Ryder – The Biography:
'Overall, this biography is a very interesting read. The chronological nature of the book is especially useful if referring back to it at a later point, and there is also a filmography and a list of Winona's awards and nominations at the back. Combined with this is a comprehensive index, making it easy to find references to particular films and people, should you wish to do so. Although it can never be as insightful as an authorised biography, or indeed an autobiography, this book is just as good as it can be. By collating information from a diverse selection of sources, Nigel Goodall has produced a good book that is well worth reading, whether you're a fan of Winona Ryder or not.'

T. J. Mackey, Dooyou Online

What's Eating Johnny Depp:

'Nigel Goodall does it again! He was the author of an estimable book about Kylie Minogue, one of the only books about the Australian pop princess to try to dig behind the myth and to get the facts right. Try to get it if you possibly can, it's called *Kylie Naked*. With his life of Johnny Depp we can see Goodall once again hovering over the glamour stars of US cinema (he has written previously on one of Depp's leading ladies, the also-diminutive trouble magnet Winona Ryder) and coming up with an intriguing portrait of a very talented man whose only trouble is corralling in all his passions. He was a teen star in Jump Street and a horror franchise, and then the director John Waters took a chance on him and cast him in his hillbilly epic, *Cry Baby*. Depp had enough smarts to say "hell, yes" to this offer and before the movie had ended audiences fell in love with his goofy charm and, of course, the shot where his pants fall off and he's left to wander in his jockey shorts. Depp showed great depth in a variety of independent and studio movies, including *Donnie Brasco*, but it wasn't until recently that he was thought of in terms of being able to "open" a movie. Throughout this checkered career (which includes a directorial debut of his own, apparently dire enough to doom a lesser man), Goodall keeps up as best he can, and both of them end up on the same page. I'm looking forward to a remake of *A Star Is Born* with Depp and Minogue, it would be utterly of the present moment...'

Kevin Killan, amazon.com

Also by the same author:

Fearne Cotton: The Biography

Ray Winstone: The Biography

The Secret World of Johnny Depp

Being Davina

Christian Slater: Back From The Edge

What's Eating Johnny Depp: An Intimate Biography

Kylie Naked: A Biography (with Jenny Stanley-Clarke)

Demi Moore: The Most Powerful Woman in Hollywood

Johnny Depp: The Biography

The Ultimate Queen (with Peter Lewry)

Winona Ryder: The Biography

The Ultimate Cliff (with Peter Lewry)

Jump Up: The Rise of the Rolling Stones

George Michael In His Own Words

The Complete Cliff Richard Chronicle (with Peter Lewry)

Elton John: A Visual Documentary

Cher in Her Own Words

Cliff Richard: The Complete Recording Sessions (with Peter Lewry)

www.nigelgoodall.co.uk

To the memory of Robert Pries

An irreplaceable, kind, generous and

brilliant individual.

'I'm a doctor. I'm a Time Lord. I'm from the planet Gallifrey and I'm 903 years old. I'm the man who's going to save your lives and all six billion people on the planet below. You got a problem with that?'

David Tennant as the Doctor (from 'Voyage of the Damned')

CONTENTS

ACKNOWLEDGEMENTS

In writing this book, my first thanks must go to David Tennant for being such an inspiration; it has been an absolute pleasure to write about your life and career so far. Secondly, I would like to thank my fabulous researchers, Keith Hayward and Mike Wilson, for coming up with so much valuable information and helping to make this book what it is – and also, Sean Delaney at the British Film Institute Library for the long out-of-circulation articles, production notes and other forgotten materials. I really must salute my very special Danish friend, Charlotte Rasmussen, whose glossary at the end of this book offers one of the best understandings for film language and film-speak that I have ever come across and deserves to be published in its own right. Further thanks to John Highfield, one of Britain's leading entertainment journalists for doing such a fabulous foreword, and also for some lively debates on the merits of celebrity, and to Sophia Nelson at 2entertain for the *Doctor Who* DVD box sets, 'Voyage of the

Damned' and the copy of David's never-before seen audition tape for *Takin' Over The Asylum*. My thanks also to Peter Zimmerman for the great author photo, exclusively shot for this book, to Chris Farley for setting it up, and to Ray James and Linda Weil for supplying the use of the Dalek. Thanks too, to Graeme Andrew for the stunning cover and brilliant design that he always comes up with, to my publisher John Blake for asking me to write this book without even seeing a proposal for it, and of course, my editors Vicky McGeown and Jane Donovan for their usual tweaking of the manuscript, and especially to Vicky for the fabulous picture research and captions. I would also like to thank the official 'David Tennant Site' on the Internet that I consulted during my research and found very useful in helping to make this work as accurate as it can be without the participation of the subject or his agent.

I would also like to acknowledge the respective January and February 2008 issues of the *Doctor Who* and *Who Do You Think You Are?* magazines that I consulted, as well as two books I am hugely indebted to: *Billie Piper: The Biography* by Neil Simpson (Blake, 2006) and *Growing Pains* by Billie Piper (Hodder & Stroughton, 2007).

Some very personal thank yous go out to the following: my sister Sue, who gave me so much new insight about my parents that it led me to examine more thoroughly David Tennant's own heritage; Cynthia Shepperd for all her years of friendship and for finding me again; and Jon Terry, a great accountant and a great friend since my amateur drama days. And finally I would like to thank all the readers around the world who have been so kind in buying my books. Thank you, thank you.

FOREWORD

BY JOHN HIGHFIELD

When Christopher Eccleston announced that he was quitting his role as *Doctor Who* after just one season as the 21st century's radically overhauled Time Lord in 2005, a whole new generation of fans reacted with shock and outrage. With Eccleston's almost sinister, brooding presence at the heart of the show, creator Russell T Davies had taken a brand that had long been consigned to the pages of TV history and transformed it into a major hit for the BBC, reinvigorating the Corporation's tired Saturday evening schedule.

But the fans really shouldn't have worried because Davies had an essential piece of Time Lord business to play with ... regeneration. So just as the show's original 1960s star William Hartnell transformed into Patrick Troughton, who then became Jon Pertwee before taking on the personality of Tom Baker — true admirers will fill you in on the names of all the subsequent Doctors — November 2005 saw Eccleston hand over one of the most coveted roles in British television to David Tennant.

A LIFE IN TIME AND SPACE

Where Eccleston had been a mysterious outsider, Tennant brought with him a truly 21st century metrosexuality, making his Doctor a winning blend of action hero and dandy, possibly the most stylish and elegant Time Lord to date. The legend is that Tennant actually became an actor because, as a three-year-old watching television at the family home in Scotland, he was inspired by *Doctor Who* of the 1970s.

He worked successfully in theatre and television for several years but it would be *Doctor Who* that saw him become one of the most famous faces in Britain, listed 24th most influential person in British media by the *Guardian*. Proving the metrosexual appeal of character and actor too, he was voted sexiest man in the universe – ahead of both David Beckham and Brad Pitt – by *The Pink Paper*, while *New Woman* ranked him at number 20 in their list of top 100 men!

With that sort of fame, of course, comes the type of media attention that his predecessor Eccleston was most eager to avoid. Star in one of the country's most popular TV dramas and you'll inevitably find the small detail of your personal life offered up for public scrutiny by the tabloids. Tennant, and his relationships with an impressive range of leading ladies – everybody from Sophia Myles to Kylie Minogue – have been the subject of their fair share of stories. The basic facts of his life have been well documented as well. From the childhood in Renfrewshire, where his father was a Church of Scotland Minister to his early days with the Royal Shakespeare Company and an extensive career in both television and film.

Now, though, comes this biography, which pulls all the stories together and sifts the facts from the tabloid speculation to present the most complete picture of the man and his work to date. Nigel Goodall has already given us biographies of some of the most influential figures in the showbiz world, including Hollywood figures like Johnny Depp, Winona Ryder and Demi Moore, home-grown celebrities including Davina McCall and Fearne Cotton and an acclaimed study of international icon Kylie Minogue.

With Tennant he faces the challenge of looking not just at the man but also at the key player in what has now become one of the BBC's most successful brands, the centre of a revitalised *Doctor Who* merchandising industry. Told with Nigel's customary thoroughness, good humour and tact, it's a fascinating investigation of both an actor and a television institution.

CHAPTER 1

BEHIND CLOSED DOORS

'I was convinced from the age of three that I wanted to be Doctor Who. Then when I discovered that Doctor Who doesn't exist I wanted to be the man who played him.'

(David talking about *Doctor Who* – 1996)

David Tennant was not in a good place. It was Sunday, 15 July 2007, and he was heartbroken. He had just watched his mother, Helen MacDonald, pass away from cancer of the colon after five years of battling the terminal illness. For an entire week, work on the *Doctor Who* Christmas episode had been suspended while he returned to his native Scotland to be with his family and to attend his mother's funeral in Paisley, Renfrewshire.

As anyone who has lost a parent will know, it was during the service itself that he found it especially hard to mask his sorrow as he paid tribute to his mother. On several occasions, as he read passages from the same copy of the Bible that Helen had been given for her twenty-first birthday, and continued to read every night during her illness, he had to pause to allow time to compose himself.

Much the same as when he joined the congregation in singing the inspirational hymns that Helen had chosen. They included Henry Francis Lyte's 'Praise My Soul, The King of Heaven', which extols the eternity of creation and the brevity of human life. David was not the only one with tears in his eyes. Many mourners shared the same sadness, especially during the singing of another of Helen's favourites, Horatius Bonar's 'I Heard The Voice Of Jesus Say, Come Unto Me And Rest'. But there was happiness, too, because Helen didn't want those who came to celebrate her life to leave the church downcast.

At her own request, the final hymn sung was 'You Shall Go Out With Joy And Be Led Forth With Peace'. And, as the congregation sang the final lines of the chorus everyone in the church clapped their hands together to create the sounds of joy and happiness that Helen had so much wanted.

As David told mourners in his final farewell to his mum, 'She wanted this to be a service of celebration and it is easy to celebrate her life.' As he led his family from their seats in the front pews down the aisle to the vestibule to thank people for coming to the service, David's father, Sandy – a former Moderator of the General Assembly of the Church of Scotland – clapped his hands and joined the congregation in singing some of Helen's most beloved gospel hymns.

During the service, Sandy thanked everyone for supporting his family in their time of tribulation – especially the Rev Lorna Hood, minister of Renfrew North, where he and Helen had made their spiritual home after 'gypsying' round other places during his lifetime in the ministry, which took him to charges like St Mark's Oldhall in Paisley and incumbencies in Edinburgh and Bathgate. He also paid tribute to the staff at Paisley's Royal Alexandra Hospital, Charleston Medical Centre and ACCORD Hospice, as well as other carers who had looked after Helen during her long fight against cancer.

Helen's committal took place at a private service at Woodside Crematorium in Paisley attended by members of her family and close friends. During her life of service to her family and community, Helen, who was highly respected for her charity work, was chair of the Paisley Friends of ACCORD Hospice. She was also a volunteer for Arthritis Care, the WRVS, the Samaritans and elderly care charity Contact.

As well as bravely sharing the reading of the Bible passages with his brother Blair and sister Karen, David spoke of his great pride in living in the light of his mother, and being part of her family: 'I will always be proud of all that Mum did, and that she made the world a better place. I am privileged to have known her and received her love. Now that Mum has gone, the world has lost a lot of its colour.'

In fact, it was tragically ironic that not long before his mother's death, David had been talking about how her illness had set his priorities straight: 'You always know that's the order of things, but when you're suddenly faced with the thought that you might lose one of your parents, that's a bit of a moment; you're never quite ready for that. That's something you know you're going to have to face, but I don't think you'll ever know what it is [like] until you face it. You just can't.'

Ten days after the funeral, David sent a personal message to his official website in appreciation of the fundraising appeal the site had organised in tribute to his mother. In his online message David thanked everyone 'for all you are doing in raising money for the ACCORD hospice in Paisley which was such an important place to my mum. It is a fantastic and worthy cause and I can't commend it to you strongly enough. The care given there to seriously ill people is of the very highest quality and my family feel indebted to them for all they've done for us. At this difficult time I can't tell you what it means that you are doing this. Thanks to everyone who has been able to make a donation. I promise you, your money will be well spent.'

Just three days before he sent that message, David had returned to the BBC set (in Pontypool, Wales – about half an hour from central Cardiff), which again, was no easy task for him. The thought of having to return to work so soon after the loss of his mother and to pick up from where he left off must have been a daunting prospect. Although the loss does not appear to have affected his performance, still it must have been a struggle throughout much of the filming. Ashen-faced, clearly still mourning, he was reportedly comforted by his co-star Kylie Minogue. The diminutive Princess of Pop had only recently returned to public life after battling her own, well-documented cancer demons and so it seemed perfectly natural that she would empathise and do the best she could to look after and comfort her colleague.

According to an undisclosed source on the set, Kylie was really sympathetic. 'She knows how terrible cancer is and she took a lot of care to comfort David. His mother's funeral was only a few days ago and he is understandably upset. She told him she understood only too well how he was feeling and what he was going through. I think he needed some sympathy on his return to work and Kylie gave him that.'

The episode that David and Kylie were filming at the time of his mother's death was the BBC Christmas Special, 'Voyage of the Damned', which saw Kylie cast as a waitress aboard the *Titanic*. Despite dreaming of a better life, she was in need of some rescuing from a spaceship of aliens by the most popular sci-fi hero in the history of British television.

Two weeks earlier, pre-production of the Christmas episode had reached the point that comes in any production when the cast and crew are called on for a read-through of the script. Assembled in the Central Baptist Church on London's Shaftesbury Avenue, this would be the first time that David would meet Kylie and probably, like most, he must have wondered what she was going to be like, quite naturally perhaps, when some of the pieces written about her over the previous twenty years or so are considered. These include speculation about her bottom being made of Teflon, as well as numerous articles about how she had fought and overcome breast cancer and was almost unmatchable as a pop star. As any pop historian or music journalist is well aware, it's hard to think of another female recording artist that has become so well loved and has reinvented herself so often, with perhaps the exception of Madonna.

In fact it was Madonna, probably more than Kylie, who was David's favourite. Obsessed since childhood, his crush on her is still much the same today as when he first set eyes on her as a teenager. 'She's quite extraordinary,' he confesses. 'When I was fourteen, the first single I ever bought was "Like A Virgin". She was kind of my sexual awakening. I had some full-on posters of her on my [bedroom] wall.' But Kylie was still a favourite and he was delighted to have her on board *Doctor Who*, even if it was just for a one-off: 'It's very exciting to have her on the show. She's part of our national consciousness, isn't she? She's as big a legend as *Doctor Who* itself, if not bigger, so it seems like a nice meeting of icons for Christmas Day.'

Kylie was taking over from the Doctor's previous companion, Martha Jones, played by Freema Agyeman, who had in the final episode, 'Last of the Time Lords' (broadcast on 30 June 2007), decided to stay on Earth so she could look after her family and finally qualify as a medical doctor. She gives the Doctor her phone so they can keep in touch and says she will see him again, but when someone is in love and it's unrequited, they have to get out, and this was Martha's way of getting out. The Doctor sets the Tardis controls, until the room is suddenly shaken with great force, and the bow of a ship smashes through the console room wall. Picking up a lifebelt, he discovers it is a lifebelt from the *Titanic*, to which he can only respond with disbelief.

Like Agyeman, who was, according to David, a delight and great fun to work with, no one could imagine Kylie ever being awkward or difficult either, but that still didn't suppress thoughts of exactly what the real star might be like to have around. Would she be nice, or would she be dull? Would she be a prima donna or even a little eccentric, perhaps? Even if she vaguely resembled any of those descriptions, no one among the *Doctor Who* cast and crew, and especially Benjamin Cook, writing for the official *Doctor Who Magazine*, could imagine her having 'a hissy fit and throwing her diamond-encrusted microphone at a roadie,' noted Cook in his article 'Star Girl' in the then new-look issue of the magazine that was on newsagent stands just five days before Christmas.

According to David (and as he told *Radio Times* when they caught up with him for their Christmas 2007 edition): '… everyone got very twittery when we heard that Kylie was coming in. At planning meetings there were all sorts of members of the art department explaining why they had to be on set. The very prospect of Kylie coming in got everyone very overexcited. Then she arrives and is refreshingly normal and fun and easy, and none of the things that I suppose a big pop diva has the right to be. She just gets on with it and is lovely to have around. I don't want to speak for her but I think she quite enjoyed being part of a team. I imagine it must get quite exhausting being your own brand. When she came in, she was just part of the gang, which hopefully was a nice thing for her to do.'

In person, Kylie is stunningly beautiful, but as anyone who has ever met her will make a point of telling you, she is tiny, and even if you are prepared for just how tiny she is, it's still a shock when you stand in front of her and stare at her famous face. True, all the trademark features are present: the disproportionately large cheekbones and teeth, the crystal-clear blue eyes and the acrobatic right eyebrow that has long been one of her favourite tools of

7

seduction. But with no make-up, no studio lights, she comes across as being simply girl-next-door and pretty rather than the glitzy image portrayed in a seemingly endless array of glamour magazine photo-shoots. Of course she is best known for her singing career, with 10 studio albums, 2 live CDs, 7 live concert DVDs and over 40 singles released internationally. All of these have been hits and have sold over 40 million records worldwide. Her first professional gig was as a child star, aged eleven, in the Australian television series, *Skyways*, eight years before she embarked on a career as a recording artist. After her seventeenth birthday, she left school to take up acting as a full-time profession.

By the time she reached adulthood, she had won five Logies (the Australian equivalent of the BAFTA) – the youngest actress ever to do so. Her character, Charlene, in *Neighbours*, back then Australia's highest-rated TV show, made Kylie a household name and she was the most popular actress ever to have come out of that soap and indeed, perhaps the most important phenomenon to have come out of Australia itself. And today, as then, her warm-hearted nature and zest for life clearly comes across and she seems impossible not to like.

Five minutes after Kylie arrived at the church hall, everyone was sitting round a table. Jane Tranter, head of BBC Fiction, started off proceedings by giving some positive feedback about the legend that was *Doctor Who* and how it had turned television into an art form. Like any read-through, whether for film, television or theatre, the cast took turns to introduce themselves to everyone: to say who they were and what role they were playing.

BEHIND CLOSED DOORS

Kylie was taking the part of Astrid Peth, a waitress aboard the *Titanic*, who would end up as the Doctor's new assistant for 70 minutes on Christmas Night 2007. The name Astrid, coincidentally, whether on purpose or by accident, was an anagram of 'Tardis'. In many ways, Kylie was playing an equally significant role as the Doctor himself. Significant, that is, when you consider the variety of roles that the Doctor's assistants have assumed over the years: from involuntary passengers, to disciples, friends or, simply, fellow adventurers. Indeed the Doctor gains new companions and assistants with almost every new series. There are some he has lost because they have returned home, or found new causes, or loves, on worlds they have visited; and then there are others, such as Kylie's Astrid, who end up dying during the course of the series or episode.

The story of 'Voyage of the Damned' picked up from where the previous series had ended. Moments after the Doctor leaves his companion Martha Jones behind on present-day Earth, the Tardis collides with the bow of the famous ship. But, as the Doctor and viewers quickly discover in the first five minutes of the Christmas Special, it isn't *the* famous *Titanic* – the historical passenger liner that struck an iceberg during its maiden voyage, on the night of 14 April 1912 and sank, 2 hours 40 minutes later, in the early hours of the following morning. Indeed no, the *Titanic* in 'The Voyage of the Damned' is a starship operated by an alien cruise line, currently enjoying a voyage to Earth to experience the Christmas holiday.

Venturing on board, the Doctor meets several of the alien tourists, and Kylie's Astrid, who is serving drinks in the entertainment lounge just before the ship is devastated by a meteor shower that threatens the lives of everyone on board, and indeed on the planet below. The Doctor hooks up with Astrid, and the other survivors, stranded in the crippled craft, to battle against saboteurs and robotic angels, armed with killer halos, in an attempt to divert the *Titanic*'s collision with Earth. As might be expected with any *Doctor Who* episode, it's a race against time as the Doctor and his companion lead a small, brave and somewhat strange band of survivors through the devastated vessel.

It probably helped the development of the storyline that *Doctor Who* writer Russell T. Davies loves disaster movies. He had, in fact, been a huge fan of the genre ever since he was snowed in during the winter of 1981, with only a copy of *The Poseidon Adventure* on VHS: 'This was in the days when a VHS was rare and exotic. I've always associated those films with Christmas because of that, but they're great templates. Battling against the odds, with epic scenes of death and mayhem all around … what could be more *Doctor Who*? Meshing that format with the Doctor's world was fascinating.'

Equally fascinating is the story of how Kylie came to be cast in the first place. Much of it appears to have been down to her creative director, stylist and one of her closest friends, William Baker. William (or 'Will', as she calls him) is, '… an absolute huge fan of *Doctor Who*. We're talking a convention-goer here! Even before its recent revival, I was always hearing about it.' Baker attended the press launch of Series Three in London on 21 March 2007, and on this occasion, according to Davies, he said how marvellous it would be to get Kylie in *Doctor Who*. The writer admits he just nodded over his glass of wine and thought, 'Yeah, yeah, not in a million years, but then he phoned up the next day and he meant it.' And to all intents and purposes, that is how Kylie ended up being cast.

Her new role was first reported in the *News of the World* in April 2007. Davies initially dismissed the story, but Baker and Kylie contemporaneously confirmed she would star in the show. Her part was officially announced on 3 July 2007. Both Kylie and *Doctor Who* had acknowledged each other before: 'The Idiot's Lantern' episode mentions the star as being a real person and William Baker included aspects of the classic series in Kylie's concert tours: the Raston Warriors from 'The Five Doctors' episode during the *Fever* tour and The Cybermen from 'The Tenth Planet' episode in her *Showgirl* tour.

If there was any disappointment for Kylie, it would have to be that she wasn't meeting the Daleks in the Christmas episode, so instead a Dalek was brought down from the *Doctor Who* set in Wales to the Worx Studio in Parsons Green, London, where she was exclusively photographed for the cover of the January 2008 issue of the official *Doctor Who Magazine* draped over the Doctor's most popular adversary.

The idea behind the photo was to recreate Katy Manning's legendary 1978 shot for *Girl Illustrated*, in which his one-time companion Katy, played by Jo Grant, posed virtually naked with a Dalek. Although Kylie was not about to go anywhere near close to being nude, or even semi-nude, she did pose, pout and show some leg in a revealing gold mini-dress that left little to the imagination. 'There was a lot of excitement when the Dalek arrived,' Kylie remembers. 'I was in the presence of a legend. I've had to gracefully accept second billing,' she joked. 'The Dalek was much bigger than I'd expected. At least I've met one now.' And perhaps, another mini-blow for Kylie might have been that she never got to hold the famous sonic screwdriver: 'I had many opportunities, but kept prolonging the moment and never got round to it.'

All the same, she was simply thrilled to have been cast, even though she wouldn't be playing a baddie, as some journalists had suggested: 'I grew up with *Doctor Who* in Australia so it's part of my childhood. I was very flattered to be invited to be part of the show, especially the Christmas episode. When I was asked to do it by Russell and Julie [Gardner, executive producer], we had a meeting over coffee to discuss what the role might be, and I just fell in love with the two of them.' It was the pair's humour, undoubted talent and passion for the show, three showbiz characteristics that Kylie clearly adores, that persuaded her and at that stage, as she explains, 'Russell hadn't written the script, so to know that he'd write it after our meeting made it all the more personal.'

Certainly Astrid came first in the writing process, confirms Davies: 'When you watch "Voyage of the Damned", you realise that there would have to be someone in Astrid's place, no matter what, but this was unusual in that we were talking to Kylie before a word had been written. But Kylie ... I never, hand on heart, expected our discussions to succeed – so I wrote the Astrid that I would have written anyway.'

The decision to cast Kylie in the first place was instinctive – as instinctive, in fact, as her acceptance. But it wasn't only the chance to work on a show as popular as *Doctor Who* that was the initial attraction, but also the opportunity to return to the medium that made her a star in the first place. 'My first day on set was like stepping back in time,' Kylie recalls. 'I felt really at home being back in the world of TV and acting. Although I had nerves, I loved the challenge of playing Astrid. It felt very liberating to be a character and not Kylie. I've definitely got the acting bug again.'

Davies admits he had no concerns about casting her: 'I knew she could act; I had no doubt whatsoever about that. We wouldn't have considered her otherwise. She threw herself into it, mucked in with everyone and attacked every single scene with energy and imagination. I can't imagine anyone playing that part better.' Nor did he worry that Kylie's iconic status would overshadow either the character or the episode as a whole: 'The show itself is iconic, and David himself such a massive and popular presence that I had no doubt that *Doctor Who* would hold its own. Once you throw in the *Titanic*, the robot host and a meteoroid storm, I swear you forget that it's Kylie.'

David was always relaxed about the casting. Admitting to humming Kylie's hits while she was on set, he also joked about filming a widely reported kiss with the Aussie star for the episode that apparently took several takes to complete. Addressing suggestions that he cheekily forgot his lines during the scene in a bid to have more retakes of the moment, he told the *Daily Record*: 'I am very professional in all things – I just go and the director tells me to stop. There were a lot of things wrong that day, it was nothing to do with me. 'Besides,' he continued, 'If you had Kylie on the show, wouldn't you have her kiss the Doctor?'

Adding fuel to the tabloids' fire was producer Phil Collinson, who also shed more light on David and Kylie's on-screen relationship: 'There's great chemistry. Kylie's character and the Doctor bond quickly in a slightly flirty way.'

Speaking at the première of the *Doctor Who* Christmas Special, 'Voyage of the Damned', when it was shown on the gigantic IMAX screen at the Science Museum in London's South Kensington, just one week before Christmas (in front of an audience that included, curiously, Peter Hain MP and celebrity chef Tom Aikens, along with *Doctor Who* alumni Camille Coduri, Noel Clarke, Shaun Dingwall, Michelle Collins and Anne Reid – though not Kylie, Catherine Tate, Freema Agyeman or Billie Piper), David was still enthusiastic about starring in the hit BBC show. 'I think it's the most exciting thing you could possibly hope to see – I'm just glad that people seem to agree. It's a very odd and slightly bewildering sort of thing to be in the middle of, but it's something that's very easy to be genuinely excited about. I really love it and even if I had nothing to do with it, I'd be looking forward to the Christmas Special, so it's a privilege to be in the middle of it all.'

High praise indeed, but there was a sting in the tail. It seemed not everyone liked the storyline. To start with, the episode was heavily criticised by Millvina Dean, the last-living survivor of the 1912 *Titanic* sinking, who thought it was 'disrespectful to make entertainment of such a tragedy.' The Christian Voice organisation was in agreement. They expressed offence at the religious imagery of a scene in which the Doctor is lifted through the ship by robot angels. But at an April 2008 conference, the unexpected happened when vicars were encouraged to use the clip, among other *Doctor Who* episodes, to 'illustrate themes of resurrection, redemption and evil' to young people.

Gareth McLean, a reviewer, who attended the screening at the Science Museum, for the *Guardian*'s TV and radio weblog, appreciated the use of 'the disaster movie template' and overall came to a favourable conclusion: 'For the most part, "The Voyage of the Damned" is absolutely smashing.' Its main flaw, in his view, was the 'blank and insipid' acting of Kylie. In echoes of the criticism that she was subjected to at the start of her career, Mclean wrote: 'She's just not that good. Truth be told, she's blank and insipid. There's no chemistry between Astrid and the Doctor, she delivers her lines with a real lack of conviction and thus we never really believe in Astrid as a character. Where Catherine Tate's Donna in last year's special was overbearing, Kylie Minogue's Astrid is hardly there at all. It does make you wonder why casting Kylie was regarded as a coup. She's a pop star – of course she's going to say yes to being beamed into millions of homes in the run-up to Christmas. She's got a duff album to sell. In truth, Kylie should be grateful to *Doctor Who*.'

According to the *Doctor Who Magazine*, in many ways 'Voyage of the Damned' was 'a kind of sci-fi murder-mystery-festive-disaster epic', that was 25-minutes too long in its first edit. 'Imagine the 1997 *Titanic* movie (the one that David calls "a bit of a rubbish film") crossed with *The Poseidon Adventure* and Kylie's 2001 on *A Night Like This* tour, which boasted a joyous mix of spectacle, glitz and glamour, elaborate ocean-liner and spaceship backdrops and young men in sailor suits.' And you will have a pretty good summation of the 2007 Christmas special

But despite what McLean reckoned, when it came to reviewing thousands of deaths over *Doctor Who*'s history, the *Doctor Who Magazine* included two of the demises from the episode in its Top 100: the death of Banakaffalata, one of the survivors of the initial collision, was placed in the 'Top 20 Tearjerkers' category, while Astrid's death was given the title of '*Doctor Who*'s All-time Greatest Death Scene'. It was, according to most viewers, 'gruesome, scary, self-sacrifice, tear-jerking, surprising, and her death would truly make a glass-eye cry.'

Although James Walton of the *Daily Telegraph* called the episode, 'a winning mixture of wild imagination and careful writerly calculation', writing in *The Times*, Tim Teeman didn't quite agree. He thought the whole piece 'sucked' and described it as 'boring'. But the *Daily Mirror* noted that it still had 'some brilliant psychedelic Pink Floyd-esque imagery, great baddies, and neat jokes', but lamented, 'the plot was a mess, consisting mostly of one hi-tech chase scene after another, and it descended into noise and bluster.' In another review, Alex Clark of the *Observer* wrote that the death toll was rather high, but he still thought the episode was, 'an oasis of cheeky nonsense and careless invention'. Harry Venning, on the other hand, concluded his positive review in *The Stage* by saying it was, '... well up to *Doctor Who*'s impeccably high standards'. The episode also received massive coverage in Kylie's native Australia, where the *Daily Telegraph* called it, 'the best-ever *Doctor Who* episode'.

But then again it didn't really matter what the critics thought.

With a viewing figure of 13.8 million, the second-highest audience for any programme during 2007, and the highest for any *Doctor Who* episode since 1979, no one should have been concerned.

As one might expect, it wasn't long after working together on the *Doctor Who* Christmas Special that Kylie and David were said to have struck up a warm rapport. So warm, in fact, reported some tabloids, that tongues had already started wagging in London. Just before Christmas, the pair were spotted making a secret visit to the Old Vic, slipping in and out of the theatre before anyone could spot them in the stalls, to watch Stephen Fry's new witty version of *Cinderella* that starred Pauline Collins as the Fairy Godmother. And if that wasn't enough tittle-tattle, elsewhere in the *Daily Mail* there were reports of the couple speaking regularly on the phone, as if they were already a couple separated only by their individual work commitments.

Even though David and Kylie remain good friends to this day, much the same as David was with Billie Piper after filming together, the stories of romance seemed somewhat far-fetched. By the time the tabloid press had suggested David and Kylie could be an item, David had already started to date Bethan Britton, from BBC South Wales, while Kylie revealed in an interview that she was also seeing someone again and even though she wouldn't reveal any name, it seemed unlikely that it might be David.

If it was going to be anyone in the public limelight, then it would probably have been her ex-boyfriend Oliver Martinez, who, like David, still remained good friends with Kylie, even after their break up. Even though rumours were in circulation that the singer had been secretly travelling to Paris in an effort to sort out her relationship with Martinez, at the time of writing reports suggest this is not the case. Apparently, the only reason she was making such trips was to see Sheba, the actor's dog. Kylie became very attached to the Rhodesian ridgeback during her illness, which ended up being featured in Kylie's 2006 children's book *The Showgirl Princess*.

Britton, on the other hand, a contracts assistant, didn't have to worry about such concerns. Going out with David would be a lot simpler than it would be if she was Kylie. For starters, she lived with her parents in a terraced house in quiet Dinas Powys on the outskirts of Cardiff. And when she met David on the set of *Doctor Who*, according to insiders, there was instant chemistry. It was November 2007, more or less a month after he had split from his long-term girlfriend, actress Sophia Myles, who he also met on the set of the show. Soon he and Bethan began seeing each other outside the show and were spending cosy nights in at his apartment in Cardiff.

In the same month that they became an item, they were in most of the showbiz gossip columns when it was reported that Bethan had been spotted sneaking out in the early hours of the morning to put a parking permit on her sports car, wearing nothing but David's pyjamas under a hooded jacket while he stood in the doorway, keeping a watchful eye until she returned.

They were also spotted on Bethan's birthday, slipping into a nearby pub for what was described as 'a romantic celebration drink'. As one observer remarked, 'They sneaked in and sat in a corner, chatting quietly. They kept a low profile but were all over each other, holding hands and giggling like naughty teenagers. They make a lovely couple.'

But four months later, they went their separate ways. Bethan was said to have grown tired of David's gruelling schedule. One of those ubiquitous friends who always seem to be on hand to comment about showbiz affairs of the heart told the *News of the World*, 'She's a lovely girl with a big heart but she was hardly seeing David because he's so busy. She became increasingly fed up spending her nights alone and couldn't see how they could plan a future together.' It probably didn't help matters that Bethan had gone public about their relationship, because if there is one thing that David hates more than anything else, it's having reporters discussing his private life on the pages of the nation's tabloids.

At the beginning of their relationship, it was obvious they really liked each other, but according to insiders at the time, 'they don't want to rush into anything too quickly and have decided to take it slowly. David has had relationships before, mainly with actresses, but their filming commitments always make it very hard to sustain a relationship. He loves the fact that Bethan has got a normal job but is still in the TV industry. They have both been hurt in the past, so they want to be careful. But the more time they spend with each other, the closer they get.'

Even when Bethan went public, and excitedly told reporters that she was seeing David and was extremely happy, it did seem like a match made in heaven: 'He's a great guy and I love being with him. It's a serious relationship; things are going well.'

But as *Now* magazine noted, David wasn't mourning the end of this relationship for long. Less than a month after splitting from Bethan, he told Denise Van Outen that he was now seeing Jennie Fava, a second assistant director, who moved to Cardiff to help film the fourth series of *Doctor Who* and had been seen leaving David's apartment in the city. The pair adopted a dressed-down look for a theatre trip to see the acclaimed revival of Peter Schaffer's *Equus* during its run at the Gielgud in London that opened that February with *Harry Potter* star Daniel Radcliffe in his first adult role playing a stable boy who has an erotic relationship with his horses. Radcliffe drew positive reviews from the critics and lots of attention from gossip columnists because of the much-written-about nude scene. Speaking of David and Fava, one onlooker remarked, 'You can tell they get on well'. Not that it would last. A few months after they were spotted at the Gielgud, the relationship that promised so much, ended up as nothing more than another of David's fleeting romances.

CHAPTER 2
THE BOY FROM THE HIGHLANDS

'I was blessed with a very good upbringing, because my parents are very moral, Christian people, but without all the brimstone and thunder nonsense.'

(David talking about his childhood – 2000)

Three-year-old David MacDonald was watching *Doctor Who* on television and he was just crazy about it. In the years to come, he would own a Tom Baker doll, have his gran knit him a multi-coloured scarf so he could run around the garden pretending to be the Time Lord and pen a school essay declaring that he would one day play the leading role.

Although many would regard a career decision slightly premature at the age of three or four, David knew, even then, that all what he ever wanted to do was to become an actor: 'I just loved watching people on the telly. I think I had a conversation with my parents about who these people were in the TV, and as soon as I had an understanding that this was a job, that people got paid for telling stories, that was what I wanted to do.'

Looking back, it was obvious that it was *Doctor Who* and in particular, Tom Baker (David's all-time favourite) that triggered his desire to become an actor in the first place, and as far as he can remember, he was never dissuaded from pursuing his goal: 'My parents expected I would grow out of it. And when I didn't grow out of it and continued to pursue it, they tried to gently suggest some other things I might want to do. They always said, "You're going to do what you want to do." But in pragmatic terms, it's a fairly stupid career. I think it's one of those things you end up doing because, for whatever reason, you feel you have to. And you feel you can't do anything else.'

As a sign of things to come, Jon Pertwee was in his second season of playing the Doctor and was only three years off regenerating into Tom Baker in the 'Planet of the Spiders' episode when David John MacDonald was born on April 18, 1971 in Bathgate, a post-industrial Scottish town in West Lothian, located between Glasgow and Edinburgh. That regeneration scene was the first time the process had been seen on screen. Suffering from fatal radiation poisoning, the Doctor is left for dead before regenerating into his fourth incarnation before viewer's eyes, rather than just taking on a different appearance as had happened with the first three Doctors.

Before all of that, of course, and before David got hooked on the programme and, like the rest of the country, ranked Baker as the most quintessential Doctor ever, he spent the first three years of his life with his older brother and sister, Blair and Karen, living in

Bathgate before the family moved to Paisley in Renfrewshire. His mother Helen was a full-time housewife, and his father Alexander ('Sandy' for short) was a minister in the Church of Scotland.

But to David, religion remains at best an abstract concept: 'I don't think, just because I'm the minister's son, that I must believe. My parents allowed me to come to my own conclusions. Let's face it, organised religion, especially in Scotland, leaves a lot to be desired and the Church of Scotland in particular has a lot to answer for. But I think I have a humanist outlook because of them – Christian in the right way.'

Sandy and Helen met at St George's Tron Church, Glasgow in 1961 when Helen was twenty-one. Shortly after that fateful meeting, she had to go into hospital and Sandy visited her there, taking along a bouquet of white tulips as a get-well gift. But according to the Very Reverend Dr James Simpson, who is today a chaplain to Her Majesty the Queen, and who conducted Helen's funeral service at Renfrew North Parish Church in the summer of 2007, 'Helen's mum was already in the infirmary, speaking to Helen, when Sandy came in with his flowers. Like most men, Sandy was a bit embarrassed about carrying the flowers, so he dropped them by the bedside and rushed out of the hospital. Helen's mum told her: "That young man is serious about you." And, soon afterwards, she and Sandy were married.' Interestingly enough, those happy days of Helen and Sandy's romance were poignantly remembered at her funeral by a beautiful bouquet of white tulips – just like the ones Sandy had courted her with – which lay on the communion table throughout the service.

Although the MacDonalds had 'gypsied' around other places in Scotland while Sandy worked for the ministry, they ended up making Paisley their home just three years after David arrived into the world, and to all intents and purposes, that is where he spent his childhood and where he was educated, first at Ralston Primary, followed by Paisley Grammar School, where he is said to have enjoyed a fruitful relationship with his English teacher, Moira Robertson, who was among the first to realise his true potential. Overall though, David remembers enduring academic studies rather than enjoying them.

What he perhaps enjoyed most was talking to his mates about wanting to become an actor and how he really wanted to play his hero, Doctor Who, which in his estimation *was* Tom Baker. Not even the emergency surgery that he had when he was nine years old, which left him battling for life with appendicitis, would deter him. 'It was certainly touch-and-go for a while,' recalls his friend Innes Smith: 'It was feared he might not make it.' On leaving the hospital, a few weeks later, he needed two months off school to allow time to recover.

It was in the period soon after the appendix scare that some pupils at his school wondered if he may be gay. He always clowned around, in and out of class, and was even a bit camp, remembers Carol Robertson: 'Loads of girls fancied him, but he didn't have many girlfriends. And so, some boys started to accuse him of being gay. But he didn't care.' And why should he? He'd already experienced his first kiss in primary school, the year after he had been signed off sick from school, with a girl called Melanie Hughes.

But that, according to David, was about four years before he started 'really' getting into music for the first time. He got into lots of Scottish groups such as The Proclaimers (still his all-time favourite band), Deacon Blue, Hipsway, The Water Boys, Hue and Cry: 'I loved all that white-boy soul thing that was going on. And also the good stadium stuff, Simple Minds and U2. I guess I was also going to the theatre for the first time, going to the Citz in Glasgow. It was an extraordinary artistic policy which they operated under; I saw some of the worst things I've ever seen and some of the best. The first thing I saw, I think, was *School for Scandal*, but an unusual, high-camp production. Brilliant! *Macbeth* set in a spaceship was probably the low point.'

The Citizen's Theatre, or the Citz, as David called it, was then, as it is today, Glasgow's very own theatre. It is what it says it is – a citizen's theatre in the fullest sense of the term. Established to make Glasgow independent from London for its drama, it produces plays which the Glasgow theatre-goers would otherwise not have the opportunity of seeing. Internationally renowned for its repertoire, it is one of few theatres in Scotland to produce its own work. By inviting a diverse range of touring work into the theatre, offers a powerful mix of productions that seal the Citizen's reputation as the place to see theatre in Glasgow.

David balanced his theatrical and musical diet with books and movies. One book that was a favourite was J. D Salinger's immortal *The Catcher in the Rye*, a novel that assumed an almost religious significance to the counterculture generation, some of whom were known to speak only in quotations from the novel. The book still resonates with readers today. Mark Chapman, the murderer of Beatle John Lennon, is one of the most notorious readers of the book. He was carrying a copy when he was arrested soon after he had shot five hollow bullets from a .38 revolver into the back of Lennon at around 10.49 p.m. on 8 December 1980, outside the Dakota Building in New York, where Lennon shared an apartment with Yoko Ono. Chapman was still reading passages from the book when the police arrived. He had apparently bought a copy of the novel from a book store in the city early that morning, a paperback edition, inside which, he scrawled 'This is my statement' and signed it 'Catcher in the Rye'.

Equally influential on David, albeit for different reasons, was actress Audrey Hepburn. 'Although I've seen lots of her films and am a great admirer of what she does, the little shrine in my head is to Audrey Hepburn as Holly Golightly. I must have been in my late teens when I first saw *Breakfast at Tiffany's*.' From an early age, he was in love: 'She has such an iconic look: the little black dress, the cigarette holder and the coquettish grin. It's a proper piece of good acting rather than the sort of slightly frothy, rom-com performance we often saw her do elsewhere. She brings that delicate, demure, butter-wouldn't-melt quality to every part, and suddenly she's playing this character who is quite dark and a bit of a loony. Yet she carries it off so assuredly you'd sell your children to get to spend some time with Holly Golightly, even though you're aware she'd be a high maintenance nightmare.

'If nothing else,' he continues, 'Hepburn makes her utterly alluring and fascinating. It's one of the great things about movies that we're allowed to indulge little fantasies about people that in life we would steer away from. She was a proper movie star in a way we're not really allowed to have these days because they have to be so exposed, and we have to know everything about them. And she was probably the most beautiful woman who has ever lived, which always helps.'

Like most of us, David probably has a mix of good and bad memories of his school years. Almost certainly, the worst times for him were the days spent at Paisley Grammar: 'I hated school, and I hated my teenage years.' The only anecdote he offers up from this period, without detailed explanation, is the night when he was beaten up. His attackers decided he was a Goth and pounced. The bullies left him to make his own way home after he was assaulted. In fact, his only fashion crime was wearing a bootlace tie in the style of Bono: 'I was spotty with greasy hair and pretty pissed-off; I couldn't wait to get to drama college so that my life could get going.'

Situated on Glasgow Road, Paisley Grammar was a non-denominational state school, which had also earned itself a bit of notoriety in 1986, the year before David left. The school was threatened with imminent closure by Strathclyde Regional Council until Margaret Thatcher, then Prime Minister, personally intervened to ensure its survival and subsequently changed the law so that local councils could no longer close schools which were more than 80 per cent full without the approval of the Secretary of State for Scotland. Naturally, the council had to abandon its plans.

Not that David had much of an interest in anything to do with politics at the time, nor with Scotland. For him, his birthplace was pretty much on an abstract concept: 'I'm very aware that Scotland is where I'm from,' he once noted. 'But I had no relationship with Scotland when I lived there. I had no interest in nationalism, no interest in Scotland's nationhood or legacy, or any of that stuff until I moved down to London, which is a terribly crass, idiotic thing to say, but it's true. My family are mostly still in Scotland, so it will always be part of who I am and what I go back to.'

But there was more to his roots than just Scotland as he would discover when he took part in September 2006 in *Who Do You Think You Are?* – the BBC's ancestry series that looks at family histories of the famous. As Sarah Williams, editor of the accompanying magazine, pointed out, the episode featuring David Tennant was fascinating because it opened up a colourful and sometimes disturbing Irish heritage.

Indeed when David started filming the programme, not only did he want to untangle his Scottish roots, but also to find out about his family in Ireland and what lay behind his grandmother's strident Protestantism. 'I guess as you get older and you look forward to the ultimate grave, you begin to become a bit more aware of your place in the scheme of things,' he conceded.

The first surprise for him came when researchers uncovered the details of the Scottish side of his family. For a start, he was no native Glaswegian. His great grandfather Donald McLeod was an immigrant to the city from the Isle of Mull. 'I've always thought of myself as a lowland Scot. The Highlands was something that I knew was there, but I'd always felt a bit of a fraud, claiming to be part of them so that was interesting to learn,' he said. 'I was keen to find out why Donald left Mull when he did, and what life was like for him – whether he left because country life was untenable or whether he came to Glasgow because he thought the streets would be paved with gold.'

The truth about Donald's motives, when it emerged at the end of one of Mull's winding country roads, was more tragic than he could ever have imagined. His family roots lay in a series of small, ruined cottages on a wind-washed hillside overlooking the sea, where Donald was one of ten children forced from their homes during the Highland Clearances in the early nineteenth century. This was the burgeoning industrial age, with wool and meat becoming valuable commodities in the new mill towns, when many highland landowners realised sheep were more profitable than tenant farmers. So they suddenly increased the rents and when tenants such as Donald's parents couldn't afford to pay, they forced them off their land and often burnt their homes to prevent them returning.

'It's the inhumanity of it that's quite bewildering,' David concluded. 'That people could do that to one another. There's also something about going and standing where it happened that brings it all home in a way that the history books just don't. There's something about seeing your mother's maiden name connected to it at such close quarters – it's quite grim, really.'

The most positive thing to come out of the trip was that when Gregory Doran, the Royal Shakespeare Company's chief associate director, watched the programme and saw David hold up and contemplate a skull exposed by renovations in the church where

Donald was baptised. He was so impressed that he offered him the role of Hamlet. 'It was like an audition,' admits Doran, who immediately sent him a text asking him outright if he had ever thought about playing Hamlet. 'He said that the two roles he really wanted to do were Hamlet and Berowne in *Love's Labours Lost*. [And as] I had already decided that I would be directing *Love's Labours Lost*, I thought it was an extraordinary coincidence.'

David's Irish connection began when his grandfather Archie, former captain of the Scottish youth football team, was signed up to play for Derry City soon after he arrived in Londonderry in 1932. By all accounts, he was a stellar success, scoring 57 goals in one season – a record that still stands today – and marrying a local beauty queen.

'Archie,' he continues, 'must have had a whale of a time. He must have thought he was in God's own country: he was a superstar and was dating a beauty queen. I'd never been to Londonderry before. I just grew up with all the reports of violence, but it seemed like such a beautiful spot, you can't quite imagine it's also a violent place.' But a violent place it was, and his family was at the centre of the sectarian struggle that has, in many ways, sadly come to define religion.

Fiercely proud Protestants, his great, great grandfather James Blair was an Orangeman and Unionist councillor. His great grandfather William was also an Orangeman and many of his family were among the 500,000 who signed the Ulster Covenant in 1912, a thinly veiled threat of insurrection if the British Government consented to Home Rule in Ireland.

Despite there being almost twice as many Protestants as Catholics in Northern Ireland due to their historical allegiance to Britain, the Protestant Irish had most of the land, money and good jobs; they also used vote-rigging – or 'gerrymandering' – to maintain the status quo. David's own family was a proud supporter of that system: 'My knee-jerk reaction was one of horror,' he said. 'I know that I'm not really qualified to judge but it doesn't really sit with my *Guardian*-reading liberalism. To me [the Orange Order] is a symbol of aggression, and certainly not of outreach and peace among men. It's quite difficult to reconcile that with the lovely people I met in Londonderry, even with my Grandad and Grandma.'

Despite his political affiliations, David's ancestor James Blair was considered something of a radical and dubbed 'a Guardian of the Poor' in a local paper. He was dedicated to social justice, fighting for better homes and wages for workers. His daughter Maisie married a Catholic, Francis McLoughlin, and their son Barry was an instrumental figure in the Civil Rights movement of the 1960s, taking part in many marches, including those of Bloody Sunday, and helping to challenge discrimination against Catholics. He also stood for election for the non-sectarian Labour party and was committed to the peaceful resolution of Ulster's problems.

'You want your family to be people you admire,' says David. 'Looking at James Blair, the whole dichotomy is there. Some things he did were admirable, yet he was mired in sectarianism. But I want to believe in what Barry believes in. I was proud to hear him talk about his ideas and his principles and [to] hear how he stood firm against becoming involved in violence, and it was good to leave a city that finally – despite everything – feels full of hope.'

He himself had that same kind of hope years earlier, when after leaving Paisley Grammar, at the age of seventeen, he successfully gained a place at the Royal Scottish Academy of Music and Drama, where he studied for a B.A. in Dramatic Arts, which covered every aspect of producing a show, whether it was for television or theatre. As part of the two-year course, the boy who wanted to be Doctor Who would learn all there was to know about movement, vocal projection, make-up, directing and stage management, and when he was through, he would be ready and qualified to go into teaching or serious acting. Even though David loved the all-consuming nature of drama school, as everyone now knows, he decided to go for the acting option: 'I liked having to fit everything in and juggling maybe three or four parts at the same time. Being slightly too busy all the time is energising and inspiring, and it was a great experience, especially because I was so green.'

It was also during his spell at drama school that he changed his name, not by choice, but because he had to – already there was a David McDonald on the Equity books. Almost by accident, he came across his new surname: 'I was on the bus looking through *Smash Hits* and I saw [Pet Shop Boy] Neil Tennant. I thought it would be a good name as it's got a good number of consonants in it,' he jokes. Not that his parents would agree. In fact, his mother wasn't at all happy about the name he had chosen. She would have much preferred it, had he taken her father's name, McLeod, or that of her mother, Blair. 'But at sixteen,' says David today, 'I wasn't having any of that.'

On leaving drama school in 1991, having already grabbed for

himself a leading part in *The Secret of Croftmore* for ITV's 'Dramarama' series, he moved onto repertory theatre, went on tour, and in between travelling the width and breadth of the Scottish Highlands, made periodic attempts to win a part in ITV's *Taggart*, a goal he somehow never managed to achieve. 'I'm the only Scottish actor alive who hasn't been in *Taggart*,' he laughs. 'Some people have been in it five times, playing three different murderers.' To overcome any disappointment he felt for not getting through any of the sixteen *Taggart* auditions he went for, he plumped for making his professional debut with the 7:84 Scottish Theatre Company in a touring production of *The Resistible Rise of Arturo Ui*.

'The 7:84 company,' David explains, 'was formed by John McGrath in the 1970s and is still going strong. It takes two or three shows a year on one-night-stand tours around the Highlands and Islands, stopping longer in the larger towns. I went for the audition just after graduating from the Royal Scottish Academy, aged about twenty – a single-minded youngster, I had started there at the tender age of seventeen – and landed the part of Giri the hitman, my first professional part. I think there can have been only about six of us in the production – I suspect for monetary reasons, rather than artistic ones. Arturo Ui was one of those Brecht plays with thousands of characters. Inevitably, we shared them all out, with the help of a few wigs and fake noses. It was great fun, we were all young and up for it. Three of us had been at drama school together and I was terrifically excited. I was fresh out of college and really rather green, but I was earning a proper wage and having enormous fun touring Scotland in a small van.

'Our first stop was Motherwell Civic Hall and the first performance was a disaster. We hadn't had time to finish the technical rehearsal, let alone attempt a dress rehearsal. We might have managed, had the production not been so complicated but we were a group of travelling players who unpacked and made themselves up on stage, so of course everyone was changing, swapping props, losing props and mislaying wigs. It was utter chaos on stage as we struggled past the point at which we had ended the technical run. I remember thinking at one point: "This is my professional debut, and it's all falling apart." But we got through it. It may have been rusty and received terrible reviews, but the whole thing had a vibrancy and energy that I adored. And of course, I thought we were excellent.'

Not so excellent was the scathing review he alone received for his second job, playing King Arthur in *Merlin* in Edinburgh. Writing for *The Scotsman*, one theatre critic was particularly chastening: 'The cast of eighteen are uniformly excellent with the exception of David Tennant, who lacks any charm or ability whatsoever.' Even though he was pretty much floored by the review, it still wasn't enough to put him off acting, or indeed, his goal of becoming Doctor Who. In fact, it was not long after the Edinburgh episode that things began to turn around when David headed down to London and moved in with comic actress and writer Arabella Weir.

CHAPTER 3

DOWN SOUTH

'I did a TV series for BBC Scotland. It was seen in England,
too, and probably every job since then has been either directly
or indirectly because of that.'

(David talking about *Takin' Over The Asylum* – 2003)

David had not worked in television since the 'Dramarama'
episode, and certainly never under his new name of David
Tennant, so when the BBC called him up five years later, in
which time he had been treading the boards in Scottish
repertory, to ask if he would like to play a transsexual barmaid
named Davina in an episode of the hit comedy series, *Rab C.
Nesbitt*, he was over the moon.

The show, which ran on BBC from the late eighties until the end
of the nineties, was one of the most underrated series of its time,
but as most critics agree, it still stands up as being one of the most
popular, funny and daring sitcoms of the 1990s. To all intents and

purposes, this was one of the key Scottish programmes being made at the time.

In the episode in which David appeared, Rab C. (played by Gregor Fisher) and his friend Jamesie Cotter (Tony Roper) are left wide-eyed and wondering when David, as Davina, pulls pints in their local. They spend the rest of the show trying to figure out whether Davina, with her long, curly, brown locks and scarlet lips, is a man or a woman until a sleazy boss, played by Andy Gray, learns the truth when he makes a pass at her.

David was only twenty-one when he filmed the episode and, undeniably, it was his first real breakthrough into television. If nothing else, it showed that he was willing to turn his hand to any kind of role in his bid for fame and fortune. Even though, as one critic pointed out, he 'scrubbed up not too badly as a woman', one cannot help wondering whether he would prefer his appearance and overall performance to be best left forgotten.

At first glance, it is probably one of the most unlikely parts that anyone would expect him to play. Much the same, perhaps, as his role as a manic depressive in the six-part Scottish TV drama, *Takin' Over The Asylum* (1994), which has now surfaced, not unexpectedly, on DVD, with David's original, previously unseen audition tape and commentary.

In a way, it was down to luck that he was cast at all. Although the show's production team auditioned actors to play the role, they still hadn't found the right person. Director David Blair, who had recently cast David in a small part in *Strathblair* soon after he had left drama school, suggested they give him a chance to audition for the part, but the casting director was unsure. After all, it was a pivotal role and there was a sense that a more experienced actor was needed to carry it off. Nevertheless the team went up to Glasgow to meet him.

The reason why the audition tape still exists to this day is down to the fact that there was no budget to fly the writer of the show, Donna Franceschild, up to Scotland with the programme-makers, so instead Blair arranged for the audition to be videotaped for her. As soon as she saw the tape, she was blown away, just as the casting director had been. David, it seemed, was on his way.

Described by *Scotland on Sunday* as 'superb, brilliantly filmed without being intrusive writing that makes you chuckle and gulp in the same sentence, and tour de force performances' it was, according to most critics and viewers, an engrossing comedy drama that explored the issues surrounding mental health with sensitivity and black humour. So applauded was the series that it won a BAFTA for Best Serial and an RTS Award for Best Writer.

The show centred on Eddie McKenna, played by Ken Stott, a double-glazing salesman, who moonlights as a DJ for hospital radio in St Judes, a Scottish mental asylum. He nurtures close friendships with the patients there, including Francine, a self-harmer, a schizophrenic played by Kate Murphy, Fergus, an electrical engineer, who has schizophrenia and later commits suicide by jumping off the hospital roof, Rosalie, an OCD sufferer for cleanliness whose son died of leukemia, for which she blames herself for not killing all the germs, and Campbell, a manic depressive played by David, with whom he shares a dream to make it onto the commercial radio scene. As Campbell's inspired antics seem to bring the pair closer to their goal, the pressures of work, relationships and family begin to get to Eddie. With his life threatening to spin out of control, now it's his turn to look for help.

It was while David was filming the latter stages of the series in the autumn of 1993, exactly a year after he appeared in *Rab C. Nesbitt*, that he met Arabella Weir, who had gone to Scotland for a week to film three episodes. Her arrival on set coincided with co-star Ken Stott's suggestion that David should move South to make a name for himself. Stott, who is today best known for his roles in ITV's *The Vice* and *Rebus*, gave him the contact details for his London agent and, after filming on *Asylum* wrapped, sent him on his way. As luck would have it, Arabella was looking for a lodger. 'So,' says David, 'I packed up my little Ford Fiesta and drove my entire life down the M6. I was terrified for the whole six-hour drive, thinking, what am I doing? It was terrifying.'

Arabella, best known as a comic performer and writer, was born in San Francisco in 1957, but she grew up in London and attended Camden School for Girls, where she says she became the class show-off. After attending drama college in the mid-1970s, she did a variety of acting jobs and was later commissioned to write for *The Fast Show*, but when she first met David in 1993, she wasn't the star-studded celebrity she is now. As he recalls, 'She seemed so laid-back and au fait with the whole thing of being on a film set. She has a very forceful personality and for a wee skinny bloke from Bathgate it was, "Oh my word, who's this?" I was scared of her, but it's all front. Once you get past that, you find she's just as insecure and nervous as everybody else, but she does have a very urbane and witty exterior.

'On set there's lots of sitting about, so you get to know people easily, and her irreverent sense of humour appealed to me. She was good fun, so I moved in [with her] for what was going to be a short time and ended up staying for five years. There's more than ten years between us now, but that never seems to have affected our relationship. When I moved down I was a young twenty-two and Arabella used to shock me with the things she would say, but she finds it harder to shock me now. She probably corrupted me, but I probably needed corrupting a little bit.'

Arabella was not an easy person to live with, it transpired, and there were times when the two 'nearly murdered each other', continued David, 'I'm sure she'll say the same about me. She has "areas of issue", rules about what goes where, which knife you use for cutting the bread and which you don't. She will freely admit that she's anally retentive to the point of bonkersdom. There was a dishwasher that we were never allowed to use, goodness knows why, and she used to have a thing about never putting the heating on. She has eased up over the years, but we used to live in near-freezing temperatures. Of course, the fact that I was from Scotland delighted her because she thought, Oh well, you're used to it, you'll be fine, so that was a particular point of conflict.

'There were other lodgers who passed through and Arabella's boyfriend eventually moved in, but I was the only constant one. I did stick with it for quite a long time, but then the rent was cheap. When I first moved in, Arry was great about introducing me to people. She was sweet, a great ally to have in a new, scary city. These days she's got children [to whose youngest he became a godfather], so there's less opportunity to see her. Her boyfriend isn't keen on the showbizzy events that she gets invited to, so occasionally I'm her date for things like that. She's generous, supportive and she's good at giving advice, particularly on relationships. She can pretty much tell you what another person is thinking. She's a loyal, warm and open person.'

But according to Arabella, when she first met David, she was on her last proper acting job while the young actor was on his first big one: 'I was completely blown away by how mesmerically talented he was. I remember thinking, Blimey, this boy's brilliant. We were shooting in Glasgow and David said, "Let's go out for a pizza tonight," and we did, and got on brilliantly. I was coming out of a not-very nice relationship and was landed with a big house in London. David was going to move to London, so I asked him to be my lodger. He did, and it was fantastic. He was a proper friend first, so there was never that "I'm his landlady and he's my serf" stuff.

'Maybe it's to do with the age difference, but it was one of those weird relationships where there was no sexual tension. He stayed on here after I met my boyfriend, Jeremy [Norton], and that was all fine. There were a few teething problems – he's not at all tidy and I'm very tidy. I'm kind of, "You're cutting the garlic with the wrong knife and don't ever cut the plastic with that Sabatier". He's kind of, "Don't stir that pasta sauce with the spoon you've just licked". And I'm more, "Don't be stupid, you kiss people you barely know".

40

'Even though, he thinks I'm finicky,' she says, 'so is he. He has to have his kiwi and his bowl of cereal in the morning. And he drove me nuts with his washing, which he'd leave in the machine for about a year. Also, I could never get him to believe that no matter how he shut the front door, to anybody inside the house it was a slam, although once Jeremy and I had babies he did get better. Ours was quite a luvvies relationship – I'd take the piss out of him for reading books about the character he was about to do, and he'd take the piss out of me for not caring about what I was doing.

'It was a very supportive relationship, though. David could, in all seriousness, stand in the kitchen and do his next big speech to me. He trusted me enough as a performer, and also as a friend. He could get quite wound-up and angsty about a part. In that situation, I'd remind him that no one actually cared about what he was doing.

'He says I've corrupted him. He was telling me a story about one of the RSC actors and I said, "David, it's not like you to laugh at that." And he said, "Yes, but you've made it impossible for me to take this sort of thing seriously." So I think, I've probably injected a good note of irreverence. David is astonishingly focused for his age, he's amazingly honest and straightforward. He's one of the handful of people I would tell a secret to and know that he wouldn't tell anybody; he's trustworthy and he's honourable. He's lovely.'

Once David had settled into Arabella's house and London itself, he very quickly became 'ridiculously fortunate' as he puts it and started to develop a career in the theatre, frequently performing with the Royal Shakespeare Company for whom, over the years, he has specialised in comic roles such as Touchstone in *As You Like It*, Antipholus of Syracuse in *The Comedy of Errors* (a role he recorded for the 1998 Arkangel Complete Shakespeare production of the play), Captain Jack Absolute in *The Rivals* and more serious parts, such as the tragic role of Romeo in *Romeo and Juliet*, Hamilton in *The General From America* and as Jack Lane in *The Herbal Bed*.

'After *Takin' Over the Asylum*, I didn't want to hang around waiting for a part in *EastEnders*,' he would smile later, remembering what his first London agent told him. 'The way to build a long career was in the theatre, and when I got into the RSC and climbed the ladder to play Romeo and such-like, I was thrilled. It was more than I could ever want, and no matter what happens to me now, I'll never regard theatre as the poor relation.'

In the same year that he moved to London, he also returned to Scotland to play with the Dundee Repertory Theatre in *The Glass Menagerie*, *Long Day's Journey into Night* and *Who's Afraid of Virginia Woolf?*, which he found to be a remarkable training ground for what he wanted to do: 'I did a whole season, three plays, one after the other, rehearsing one during the day and performing in another that evening. It was great because I got to play parts that I might not naturally have been cast in.' But it was, he continues, 'when I got my first job at the National that I was over the moon. That was further than I ever thought I'd get.'

The bad news for David, however, being at the Royal National Theatre in London and playing the role of Nicholas Beckett in Joe Orton's *What The Butlar Saw* was that he would have to appear near-naked on stage. It was something that he had not done before, not that he seemed worried: as far as he was concerned, it was simply part of the job.

The play consisted of two acts and revolved around Dr Prentice, a psychiatrist attempting to seduce his attractive prospective secretary, Geraldine Barclay. It opens with the doctor examining Miss Barclay in a job interview. As part of the process, he convinces her to undress. The situation becomes more intense during Dr Prentice's supposed 'interview' when Mrs Prentice enters, and he attempts to cover up his activity by hiding the girl behind a curtain.

His wife, however, is also being seduced and blackmailed by Nicholas Beckett, played by David. She therefore promises him the post as secretary, which adds further confusion. Soon, Geraldine is dressed like a boy and Nicholas is dressed as a girl, Winston Churchill is missing body parts and the doctor digs himself further and further into trouble by piling up more and more ridiculous lies. Dr Prentice's clinic is then faced with a government inspection. Led by Dr Rance, the inspection reveals the chaos in the clinic and Rance, who talks about how he will use the situation to develop a new book, which he says will bring together incest, buggery, outrageous women and strange love-cults.

When the original production of the play was staged at the Queens Theatre in Shaftesbury Avenue, London in March 1969, almost two years after Orton was brutally bludgeoned to death by his ex-lover Kenneth Halliwell, with nine hammer blows to the head, there were some cries of 'Filth!' from the gallery, but the work was still considered enjoyable, even if it was, as some critics noted, a somewhat staid revival and survived as a largely shock-free Swinging Sixties period piece.

If David never thought he would get so far as to walk the boards at the National, perhaps he was equally surprised that year when he also landed a bit part and shared a scene with Christopher Eccleston in Michael Winterbottom's big-screen adaptation of Thomas Hardy's tragic *Jude*, a profoundly moving drama unrelentingly bleak in its depiction of love and poverty in the late-nineteenth century. Although it was the only time that he would share any on-screen time with Eccleston, it was, of course, from him that, nine years later, he would take over his childhood fantasy role of playing the key role in *Doctor Who*.

When he wasn't working in theatre or film, David filled his schedule with bit parts on television. He appeared in such popular shows as *The Bill*, *Randall & Hopkirk (Deceased)* and *Foyle's War*. Appearing so much on television in those days, even if it was only small parts, probably helped him to familiarise himself with the technical side of film-making because it hadn't been part of his drama school training. Filming was not like acting, so yes, he admits, 'I had to [learn] because it wasn't part of my course then. There are all sorts of terms [like rolling, speed, slate, action] that can throw you if you don't know them when you start out, but I found that film crews were always happy to help. You learn a bit about editing too, along the way, learning to save your best performance for a close-up and not a wide shot, that kind of thing. It's about getting the right emotional state as raw as you can make it on the right take, which is just something you get right with experience.'

Part of that experience is learning how to get into character and becoming thoroughly acquainted with the story, something that's hard for anyone when the tale keeps shifting, when the plot, continuous on paper, suddenly flies to all points of the compass, only to be reassembled much later on the cutting-room table. Even if it's all part of the process, it must sometimes become tedious: from the early hours of the morning till late at night, watching scenes laboriously set up over hours of preparation, only to have them cut short or cut with barely a word spoken.

David also had his own technique for reaching an emotional point in a scene: 'You need to take yourself by surprise a little bit. If you need to listen to a certain piece of music, for example, as a trigger, I think your reaction stops being potent. I personally just need a bit of quiet. But you know, there are no rules. If it works for you, then you should do it.'

But there is also a need, he admitted, to find time to wind down in between takes: 'You need to be able to relax as filming days are long, often starting at six in the morning and going on until eight at night. You can't be primed every second, you'd kill yourself by week three. You need to chill out, but be ready to take the time you need to prepare for a challenging scene. It's all about choosing your moment: knowing when to get a bit of space to prepare and knowing when you can just have a chat or read the paper.'

CHAPTER 4

BRIGHT, LIGHT CITY

'Making the film in Los Angeles – with English producers, a Finnish director, French money and American cast – was fantastic and absurd.'

(David talking about *LA Without A Map* – 2000)

By the summer of 1998, David had moved out of his lodgings with Arabella and Jeremy, and had found himself a flat of his own in North London. Not that he would have much time to settle into his new retreat – soon after he moved into the new home, he left for Ireland to commence work on his first major film role for Deborah Warner's directional film debut, *The Last September*. Eventually it was premièred during the official selection of the 'Director's Fortnight' at Cannes during the film festival, the following year.

Although he had already appeared in *LA Without A Map*, and wasn't at all surprised at its failure to set the box-office alight, he was proud and ecstatic about his role in *The Last September*, and indeed about the movie's overall attraction. 'It's based on a novel by Elizabeth Bowen and set in Ireland in 1920,' he said. 'It's shades of Merchant-Ivory, but I think a bit grittier than that. I play a British army officer, who's there helping to protect a big house owned by an Anglo-Irish family. I fall in love with the daughter of the house, played by Keeley Hawes, and she sort of falls in love with me, but can't make up her mind between me and the IRA man hiding in the woods. So you have the political side of it, which is fascinating.' The storyline was something he admitted to knowing very little about.

The idea for the film was the brainchild of Neil Jordan, who brought the screenplay to Deborah Warner and encouraged her to read the novel. It was the first time that Warner had read any of the writer's work but when she did, the whole thing blew her away. What she liked so much about it was how, 'it was like something so beautiful that it hurts. Bowen explores the tightrope between the surface of how people present themselves and their seething, boiling emotional worlds beneath. With seeming effortlessness, she combines this intensity with a meticulous observation of social comedy.'

As online critic James Berardinelli noted, '*The Last September* is a brooding, moody motion picture with a powerful atmosphere that emphasises the sense of encroaching doom. This is the kind of story that cannot end well. Like *The Garden of the Finzi-Continis*, the film explores the mindset of a group of people who will not acknowledge the impossibility of remaining apart from the turbulent, changing world around them. Eventually, the violence will reach into their lives and their home.'

The tale revolved around the impending end of an era and an autumnal sense of loss hangs over everything. Halcyon days are past, darker seasons are coming. The time frame is the early 1920s and the location is County Cork, Ireland. Hostilities between the Irish Republicans and the British are growing. Caught in the middle of all this is the so-called Anglo-Irish, those British citizens who moved to Ireland decades ago to oversee the country, who now consider themselves Irish. Many of the locals, however, still view them as foreigners, in part because they have refused to give up the traditions and customs of their native land. As a result the Anglo-Irish find themselves in a difficult hybrid situation, not belonging fully to either side, thus earning a measure of distrust from both.

Although the film picked up a Golden Frog nomination for Cinematographer Slawomir Idziak at the Camerimage International Film Festival of Art of Cinematography, in the end, it didn't walk away with any awards. As David has since suggested, if it had been a foreign film, 'it would have won all the awards going'. It seems strange that it went completely unappreciated amid the plethora of awards shows with which Hollywood and Britain now abounds.

By the time *The Last September* was on general release, following its debut in Cannes, David had met and was dating Anne-Marie Duff, whom he had met while working together in *Vassa: Scenes from Family Life* at the Albery Theatre in London in January 1999. They first became close during rehearsals and at the time David declared her to be 'the nicest person' he had ever worked with. Their relationship soon blossomed into something deeper and, a year on,

Anne-Marie admitted, 'I'm in love. I'm walking around with a sunshine burst around my head.'

Directed by Howard Davies, *Vassa* was comic portrait of a powerful matriarch, a woman of iron will, played by Sheila Hancock, who sees her family destroyed by the very values that she seeks to preserve. David played the crippled Pavel, what the *Daily Telegraph* called 'a flesh-creepingly horrible creature', the type you know you ought to feel sorry for but 'the hunchbacked little nerd snivelling self-pity repels all sympathy'. Anne-Marie was cast in an equally 'nasty' part as a spiteful young mistress.

Although the play didn't set their careers alight, it did bring them together for what was said to be a very ideal four-year relationship. Anne-Marie still believes to this day that opposites really do attract. At the time of being involved with David, she said, 'My flat is very messy, while his is neat and pristine. I think I'm quite good at loosening him up, so that balances things.'

Interestingly enough, it was not until after they split up in 2003 that their respective careers would rocket sky-high through the showbiz roofs. Duff eventually took the part of Fiona in Channel 4's *Shameless* while David, of course, ended up fulfilling his childhood dream of playing Doctor Who. Unlike many other couples that break up, they remain close friends to this day and although no explanation was offered to the reason of why they parted company, it was perhaps a little ironic that the year after they did they appeared together in the stage production of John Osborne's love triangle, *Look Back in Anger*, playing husband and wife. Nor was it surprising that David was attracted to her. By all accounts she was exactly the type he liked. Slim, petite, with blue eyes and blonde hair.

Even though *The Last September* managed to strike more of a chord with audiences than *LA Without A Map*, David saw no reason to regret his decision to accept the role. In the film he played Richard, who has his life turned upside down during a burial in a Bradford cemetery, when he meets Barbara, a beautiful young actress from Los Angeles. Leaving behind his inherited undertaker's business and the well-meaning girlfriend he was destined to marry, Richard crosses the Atlantic in pursuit of love, adventure and a screenwriting career. As an Englishman abroad, he finds himself in situations that are very funny viewed from afar, but may prove tragic close-up.

Starring in a Hollywood film and filming there for three months must have seemed like another dream come true when you consider that David, although already regarded as a theatre veteran even in those days, was in many ways still learning his craft when it came to working in front of a movie camera. Up until then his only previous outing onto a film set had been one day's work on *Jude*. But, as he would later point out, when he described the LA scene: 'Everyone is so wired-up and slightly artificial the whole time. There are some lovely people, but it's quite hard just to be normal; it's such a culture shock. I think that would drive me mad after a while – if I was going to live there, I'd need to have some really good pals that you could just go and hang out with, and just be normal.

'Luckily,' he continued, 'I had a friend with whom I was at

drama school and who is out there now. It was good to have him there just to have a bit of a touchstone to reality.' Nowhere was that more needed than on the film set itself – everywhere David went, a minder would follow him, just to carry his personal chair ...

'They do look after actors terrifically well in LA, almost *too* well – the big trailers and all that kind of business are the norm. And you get followed about with these chairs everywhere you go. You think, please don't follow me about, it's very embarrassing. If I want to sit down, I can sort myself out. But they're adamant about it. They're like, "I have gotta do this, this is my job. If I don't follow you with this chair, I am out of here." It's terrible.'

Perhaps the only breath of fresh air during filming was the producer and director, Mika Kaurismaki. He was, according to David, 'very keen that there were no "favoured nations" as he called it. So we all got exactly the same kind of treatment.'

Of course the icing on the cake was when he later learned that Johnny Depp would be making an appearance and would be sharing scenes with him: 'In a sense, Johnny was doing a favour and he enjoyed coming in and doing his little cameo. When Johnny came on the set, there was a definite air of muted hysteria going on. He is a huge international star and there's no reason why they shouldn't get excited about it. But he is decidedly down-to-earth, very laid-back about it all.'

Even more surprising, perhaps, was how David actually ended up hanging out, off-set as well as on, with Johnny. One of those times was when his fellow actor introduced him to the now-famous Viper Room, the nightclub situated on the corner of

Larabee Street and Sunset Boulevard, that Johnny had bought with rock star Chuck E. Weiss back in the late summer of 1993. More fatally, it was where River Phoenix, by then one of the most significant actors of his generation, collapsed and died on Halloween morning that same year, on the pavement outside the club, from a fatal cardiac arrest caused by a lethal cocktail of drink and drugs.

As soon as Johnny got his hands on the club, he arranged for it to be refurbished for what was for him, a characteristically 1920s speakeasy around which the rest of the décor would subsequently revolve. Even the cigarette girls that he hired were a throwback to the period, as was the tiny centrepiece dance floor surrounded by five equally tiny booths, one of which was permanently reserved for Johnny's agent, Tracey Jacobs, with a 'Don't Fuck With It' gold plaque as if she was the Hollywood equivalent of Elvis Presley's notorious manager, Colonel Tom Parker.

As Parker's biographer, Alanna Nash, points out, 'Whether regarded as a meretricious and evil confidence man, or as a brilliant marketer and strategist, Parker was as remarkable as the star he managed. No figure in all of entertainment is more controversial, colourful or larger than life.' Whatever secrets Parker may have harboured or taken to the grave with him, he remained loyal to Elvis for the whole time that he was his manager and almost always fought hard to preserve Presley's image. Although no one could confirm if Jacobs was even close to that description, it does provide food for thought.

As David described, 'The security was fierce and the bouncer couldn't find my name amongst this sheet of around twenty bits of paper. He was telling me I wasn't on it and I was praying that Johnny had put me on the list. It would have been so embarrassing as there was this massive queue of people, all trying to get in. But eventually the guy found it and I ended up rubbing shoulders with Hollywood for a night. It was fantastic.'

Like most people working with Depp for the first time, David naturally found it somewhat intimidating, but 'he immediately put me at ease. So much so that I ended up doing these scenes with one of the biggest stars in the world and not really realising it. We got on very well.'

Although David still describes his first Hollywood experience as 'fascinating', he couldn't wait to get home to London: 'I feel fiercely loyal to Scotland and, slightly absurdly, you tend to become terribly nationalistic when you move away. Only then do you realise what it is to have a country that has a strong national identity, which I don't think England does. But I like the bigness of London. Because actors tend to end up here, I've got a lot of friends from back home who are now down here.' Nor would he allow the experience of his breakthrough in Los Angeles to go to his head, being only too painfully aware that, 'In a profession like this, there's always a lot more steps up and a lot more steps down.'

Filming in Britain, however, was not so straightforward as shooting in and around Hollywood. It was very strange, David noted: 'We started filming here on Monday and it's like a whole new crew – most of the actors are new here, it's like starting on another job; it's very weird. We were in America for three-and-a-half months, so we've done most of the film. We're in Bradford for five days, and then it's all over. I've not done a big movie before – for me it's been a bit of an eye-opener.'

Much the same as it was for his director Kaurismaski – but for different reasons. After the California sun, where most of the $4.2 million movie was shot, he wanted a typically gloomy, overcast Yorkshire morning for the funeral scene, but he was unable to get what he had in mind. The unseasonably good conditions that January meant that he had to re-schedule the day's filming and jump from where he had set the shot up on a hill above Bradford to the city centre, where interestingly enough, Tom Courtenay's *Billy Liar* had been filmed, 35 years earlier.

No sooner had work on *The Last September* finished than David started on another film. More than likely, he would have been feeling pretty pleased because since he had moved down to London, he had not really suffered any long periods of being without work. Maybe a couple of months here and there, he said, but on the whole he had nothing to complain about: 'Not getting work is the thing about our job which is rubbish – you can't do it on your own. I think the only thing to do is to keep positive and try not to watch *Countdown*,' he laughed. 'Fill your days, otherwise you'll go mad. I've sometimes taken jobs just to keep working because I hated not working, but that's not the best way for everyone and sometimes it's right and proper to turn things down. It's just I've never really done it!'

One offer he certainly wasn't about to refuse was the audition that he attended for Stephen Fry's directional debut, *Bright Young*

Things. The audition, unlike some he had been to, was very straightforward. As he explained, 'Stephen is an actor himself and so I think he didn't want to torture us with a long, drawn-out process.' David won the role of Ginger Littlejohn on the film.

Bright Young Things was an adaptation of Evelyn Waugh's classic 1930 comic novel, *Vile Bodies.* Set in London between the world wars, the tale frantically follows a group of socialites as they literally invent youth culture and partake in the delights of what passed for decadence in that period: primarily drug-use and busting gender conventions at extravagant theme-galas. With a backcloth of nightclubs, dancing, jazz and speed, their lives revolve around an endless series of parties and pleasure seeking: motorcars, jazz bands, gossip journalism, drugs and gramophones. Inevitably, the frantic pace of living takes its toll and one by one, they begin to crash and burn in the search for newer and faster sensations.

Although this was largely an ensemble piece which follows several storylines similar to Robert Altman's 2001 masterpiece, *Gosford Park*, the central characters are young writer Adam (played by Stephen Campbell Moore) and his love, the aristocratic, but unfunded Nina (Emily Mortimer). Like the other bright young things, Adam and Nina are radically flippant in all matters – and to one another – but their cheerful lack of any kind of concerns plainly conceals much deeper emotions. However, practicality eventually seeps in and Nina, having never received a sincere declaration from Adam, and with no means of support, abandons him for another.

Although some critics considered the film to be 'overly

cluttered', most adored the work beyond words. *Company* magazine declared it, 'A delicious cocktail of glam costumes, eccentric characters and hilarious one-liners'. 'This is a gem of a movie and a welcome treat,' agreed Natasha Poliszczuk, writing for *InStyle* magazine, 'A delightful whirl of a movie that fizzes with energy and poignancy. Look out for sparkling cameos from Brit flick stalwarts.' In another rave review, *Screen International* described it as the renaissance of British entertainment: 'Fry has captured all the anxious, frazzled spirit of Evelyn Waugh's novel *Vile Bodies* in an exuberant directorial debut. A polished affair, this star-studded, social satire will appeal to the same sophisticated audience who journeyed to the cinema for *Gosford Park*. Breathless, fast-paced and very funny.'

Probably the last thing in the world that David expected after *Bright Young Things* was to end up being cast in the BBC adaptation of Anthony Trollope's, *He Knew He Was Right*. Most critics agreed that his portrayal of Mr Gibson, the vain and creepy vicar, intent on marrying upward, was pitch-perfect. The story centred round a young married couple whose relationship is torn apart by the husband's jealousy and obsession with rumours that his wife has had an affair. He refuses to believe her denials and descends into a terrible depression. David's character provided some welcome light relief to the story, with a comedy turn as the vicar forced to choose between two sisters, neither of whom he really wishes to marry. The *Hollywood Reporter* called it, 'Comfort television of the highest order: intelligent drama, well acted with crisp dialogue and all the ingredients required for a period piece. Richly atmospheric ...'

Perhaps an even greater surprise was when he was recruited for what would turn out to be his first headlining prime-time BBC television drama, playing one of the three principal characters. Peter Bowker's *Blackpool* was a six-part musical drama about the murder of a young man in a Blackpool arcade and how it affects those involved in the arcade and in the investigation.

'I got sent the script and I thought it was brilliant,' he enthused. 'I had to get a part in it. The writing was really good – it wasn't just the gimmick of the songs. It was so unusual and so out there.' It was one of the things that always grabs him: 'A script just works, or it doesn't, it's something chemical. Good writing just is – it's difficult to define. Sometimes it's something that plays with a role so much that it shouldn't work, but it does. The story has to take you along and the dialogue has to sound like someone is really speaking it; you just know. That first pure reaction is quite an important one.'

With this particular piece, he knew from the outset: 'I loved it. It's so different and so exciting. It's great writing, it's great storytelling, but also with this wonderful device – the songs and the graphic sequences, and the fact that it can move from fantasy to reality and it seems to do so very easily. It's brilliant to have a prime-time drama that's so different, and so brave. It's really difficult to describe the drama. I think that's good, though, because it means you can't categorise it. It's everything, really. It's a family drama, a whodunit, a rite of passage, a love triangle, a musical.'

Whatever category it actually fell into, *Blackpool* was the story of Ripley Holden, played by David Morrisey, an ambitious, bullying arcade owner, who believes strongly in luck and is planning to turn his arcade into a Las Vegas-style casino hotel and thus revive Blackpool's fortunes. DI Peter Carlisle, played by David, is the investigating officer of the murder. He is a charming and good-natured, although extremely manipulative, police officer, who dislikes Holden almost on sight. Natalie Holden (played by Sarah Parish) is Ripley's shy, frustrated and lonely wife, whom he takes for granted and to whom Carlisle takes a shine.

As the murder investigation proceeds, it takes its toll on all the characters. Ripley is under suspicion of murder and soon finds his public and private life slowly unravelling, as both his bullying nature and long-forgotten demons from the past return to haunt him, while Carlisle, intent on proving Ripley is the murderer and planning to use Natalie to get to him, finds himself genuinely falling in love with her. Certainly, from day one Carlisle has it in for Ripley. He takes an instant dislike to the man he's investigating on suspicion of murder, while being simultaneously attracted to the suspect's wife.

Although at the time David took pains not to be drawn into his character's principles, he confessed that it was 'completely and utterly inappropriate' for Carlisle to have an affair with a murder suspect's wife. 'I won't make moral judgements on the character, though – I don't think that's my job, really,' he laughed. DI Carlisle has been called in to help out the Blackpool Constabulary when a body is found in Ripley Holden's showpiece arcade. As soon as he meets the hapless entrepreneur, he thinks he's found his man, but does he believe that Ripley actually committed the murder, or is he simply out to get him?

'I think it's a bit of both,' David noted enthusiastically. 'He develops an instant dislike of Ripley, just because of who he is and his arrogance, and he decides that Ripley's the man. But that's compounded by the fact that Carlisle ends up compromising himself, so it becomes convenient for Ripley to be guilty too, and it becomes an emotional and sexual thing to nail Ripley. I imagine Carlisle is usually very full of integrity and rather good at his job but, for the first time, he finds himself on the slippery slope to madness.'

Even if in retrospect, David's fascination with the role he was playing certainly wasn't characteristic of his favourite kind of part, the musical aspect of the story hit a high note and appears to be an aspect of the character that he found most challenging. Although he'd had some training in singing and dancing at drama school, it wasn't something that he had done a great deal of. Of course he had experienced the 'basic stuff', as he calls it, but it was nothing like the challenge he now faced. Soon after filming was completed, he admitted that yes, it had been fun 'dusting down some half-remembered half-skills.'

Certainly, there were not many roles around that would offer him the opportunity to enjoy such experiences as dancing underneath Blackpool Prom in the dead of night: 'We've found ourselves doing some quite unusual things, like being in a pool fully clothed, or dancing the tango with David Morrissey to "These Boots Are Made For Walking". And we found ourselves at 3.00 a.m. in the concrete colonnades underneath Blackpool Prom, dancing to The Smiths. It's been eye-opening and invigorating to get to do all of these things at once.'

Indeed, for David, it was The Smiths' track, 'The Boy With The Thorn In His Side', that was the most fun: 'That was the biggest number for me – I had to learn the most dance steps for that one. It's a full-on number with 25 dancers and the actors; it's quite scary. And because you're playing the character, so you tend to be at the forefront of the scenes, but you're surrounded by these dancers who can all do it, and you've got to sing at the same time and act as well ... and keep up the psychological thing with the characters, so it's been interesting. I also love the Elvis Costello track that's in it, "Brilliant Mistake", and there's a great song by The Faces called, "Ooh La La" – which I didn't know, but it's lovely.'

As far as he was concerned, the only track that was missing was one by his favourite band of all time, The Proclaimers. No matter how hard he tried, he just wasn't able to persuade Peter Bowker to include '500 Miles'. 'I was desperate to get some Proclaimers in,' he laughed. 'I'm a big fan and have been for ever. It would have fitted my accent as well – everything else you have to sing with an American accent, so it would've been nice.'

To complete six hours of television one assumes that the *Blackpool* production crew must have spent the best part of three months in the seaside town, with its distinctive 'Pleasure Beach' and omnipresent smell of deep-fat fryers. But the truth, says David, is that they didn't spend that much time there: 'Typically the BBC was saving money, so basically any shot that didn't have the tower in the background was probably not shot in Blackpool. We filmed there for about four weeks out of the twelve weeks of shooting.'

The show first became noticed because of its unconventional use of music, as Bowker featured popular songs as a dramatic device. When Carlisle arrested Ripley's son for handling drugs, for example, the characters suddenly broke into Morrissey's 'The Boy With The Thorn In His Side', complete with a choreographed dance routine. The emotion of the moment was thus relayed far more efficiently than mere words alone could convey. 'It was deceptively tricky to make it work when we came to do it,' continues David. 'Initially we were just miming but then we went back and recorded our own voices so that you actually had the two voices together. We all resisted it and we were brought, kicking and screaming, to the recording studio. It wasn't using music in the same way that Dennis Potter did – we were using it like a stage musical, it was very much part of the action whereas Potter used them as fantasy bubbles, really. By taking out our actual voices it made it become fantastical. It was a learning process for everyone involved in making it work.'

But *Daily Telegraph* critic James Walton was unable to see the point of their dramatic purpose: 'It wasn't even clear whether the singers knew they had sung them – or whether the songs were meant to represent the unsaid.' All the same he liked it, as did most other critics, especially when the first episode began with Morrissey and Parish singing along to Elvis Presley's 'Viva Las Vegas': 'Unlike in Dennis Potter, when the characters join in rather than lip-synch, after two tunes along the way it ended with Carlisle and Ripley performing "These Boots Were Made for Walking". All four were big production numbers that added to the good-natured, anything-goes atmosphere.'

Blackpool was nominated for the Best Drama Serial award at the 2005 BAFTAs, and won Best Mini Series and Grand Prize accolades at the Banff Television Festival in Canada. It went on to become a huge success for BBC America, where it was renamed *Viva Blackpool* and received nominations for Best TV Mini Series at the prestigious 2006 Golden Globes. It seemed David had reached a tipping point.

As Peter Bowker noted, one of his greatest talents is to be 'ugly and handsome in the same scene. David can go from geeky copper to handsome lover in just one moment and I think he knows when he's doing it – that's the sign of a great actor. He's very good at capturing those moments when you find yourself surprisingly drawn to someone emotionally.'

Blackpool also meant that David was now being recognised in the street and that was when he started to get autograph-hunters: 'It was men of a certain age, asking what it's like being in bed with Sarah Parish.' Even though there were rumours that their relationship wasn't purely restricted to the screen, David wanted to keep his private life private. In fact, he is known to be notoriously private, preferring to maintain a comparatively low profile whenever he can: 'No one teaches you how to deal with all that sort of stuff. You have to decide for yourself where the line will be drawn. It's about your own personal integrity. You just have to figure it out as you go along,' he explained.

And fame, he insists, has never been something that he has chased: 'It takes a bit of getting used to, it's a bit weird the first time a photographer chases you down the street, but it's churlish to complain about it. I like being recognised for what I do and I'm proud of what I do – being a well-known actor is a very privileged position. I don't talk about my private life, I choose to define my own boundaries and not take every available publicity opportunity. I don't think I would have coped very well at twenty-one, so I'm glad I've had a few years working first before dealing with being famous.'

CHAPTER 5

THE DREAM COMES TRUE

'I got *Casanova* in a very traditional way, just through auditioning. I read a couple of scenes, got called back, read them again, and then got the job.'

(David talking about *Casanova* – 2005)

Four months after *Blackpool* was screened on British television, the *Media Guardian* named David as one of the faces to watch. The success of *Blackpool*, with its 5 million viewers in the UK and as *Viva Blackpool* on BBC America in October 2005, firmly established him among the rising stars of the day. Although the general public still had only a passing familiarity with him, he was nevertheless being tipped as the next great performer to follow Ewan McGregor, Dougray Scott, Robert Carlyle and John Hannah from North of the border to succeed in finding an international audience.

Perhaps much of the appeal comes from the fact that he is boyish, electric-thin and very much a modern kind of leading man. He retains a sort of undergraduate quality, and what he lacks in chiselled jaw and shoulder span, he more than makes up for in the animation of his face and his quick intelligence. It's easy to see why smart casting directors have spotted his appeal for women in direct contrast to the more traditional, slab-like leading men of old.

It probably helped that he was about to be seen in the second of his two significantly major television dramas of the period. *Casanova*, produced by the same team who brought *Doctor Who* back to the fore, was a three-part serial which premièred on BBC3 in March 2005 and was repeated, just a few weeks later, in a primetime slot on BBC1.

Production started in October 2004, in and around Manchester, and on location in Dubrovnik and Venice, where interestingly enough, the serial was given the alternative nickname of 'Little Casanova' due to Swedish director Lasse Hallström, best known at the time for *The Cider House Blues* (1999), filming his own version of the story with *Brokeback Mountain* star Heath Ledger for cinema release just over a year later. Although the productions were in town sharing the same facilities, it was when the city flooded during the making of both TV drama and Hollywood epic that 'Big Casanova', as it was called, was put on hold. In contrast, the BBC gang simply strapped plastic round their trousers and got on with their version.

The idea of making the series was originally developed for ITV by Michele Buck, Damien Timmer and Julie Gardner (before she moved from London Weekend Television to become head of drama for BBC Wales). 'There was an over-commitment to period drama at ITV at that time,' noted Buck. 'The natural home for the project was the BBC as Jane Tranter had the vision to realise it in its larger format.' Tranter, BBC controller of drama commissioning, couldn't agree more: 'While the ITV network wanted *Casanova* to be a single piece, we were keen to do what Russell wanted to do – to make it a more expansive, three-part serial journey, which is raunchy, modern and relevant.'

In fact, Russell T. Davies was very excited about it: 'I took this as a chance to reinvigorate period drama and to tell a dazzling and very funny story. We're bringing back to life, for three hours, a truly remarkable man and a genuine legend. When I sat down to read Casanova's autobiography – all twelve volumes of it! – I discovered that our modern-day impression of a lascivious, misogynist man is hopelessly wrong. He's been filtered down through the centuries as a bastard. I wanted to rescue him, to show what he was really like. This man genuinely loved women and respected them with an astonishingly modern mentality. And never mind the serial shagger, I also discovered that, outside his love life, Casanova was a wonderful, barmy, inventive man.

'In many ways,' he continues, 'He was like an eighteenth-century Jeffrey Archer, but with a difference. He wasn't born an aristocrat, but like Archer, he lied his way into jobs and positions of power with charm and cheek – he was just irresistible.' Above all, Davies wanted *Casanova* to offer a fresh take on the world's greatest seducer and so he went all out to make it into a fast, funny and sumptuous production, with all the resources the Corporation could muster and with David taking on the role of the young Casanova, while Peter O'Toole played the same character in his later years.

Not that the story meant much to David: 'To be honest, I didn't really know much about Casanova. My first experience of him was reading Russell's script, which wasn't what I was expecting. In the script he's not a lothario and he's not really a ladies' man, he's just someone who's passionate about the women he's passionate about. He's not sneaky or conniving, or dishonest to any of them. Obviously, there was something really likeable about him. He wasn't a nasty piece of work, he was just somebody who existed on his instinct. And the character that hopefully we're portraying is someone who absolutely drinks the dregs of life of every experience that he can.'

Davies also wanted to make sure that the correct choices were made with the casting so that his new version would be completely different to anything that had gone before. After sitting through countless tapes of actors strutting their stuff, when he reached David's tape, he knew instinctively that finally he had found his Casanova: 'The minute his audition tape started, I just went, "Oh, that's it!" I'd thought when I was writing *Casanova* that if he's just handsome, it makes all the women in the script stupid. Being sexy is not just about good looks and he walked that audition.

'Not only that,' he continues, but 'he was funny, not in a slapstick way, and that's one of the keys to the character. David's not your classical screen god, instead he's interesting and intelligent, with a lightness to his acting not many straight actors have. And, as with Casanova, he certainly does seem to have an effect on all the women around him.'

David, of course, was thrilled with the new challenge. Even

more so, because at first he really didn't think he would land the role. 'I didn't expect to get Casanova at all,' he recalls. 'When I saw the list of people up for it, I thought it would go to [one of] the "Beautiful Boys".' 'Beautiful' is not at all how he sees himself. 'I genuinely don't think I am,' he said at the time. 'I've never read anything that suggests I might be … I think that's precisely why I got Casanova, because they didn't want that, they wanted him to be a cheeky chappie – that's why his love rival is Rupert Penry-Jones, who's 6ft 2in. It was all about the wit and the words.'

He was equally delighted when a journalist suggested he was technically the young Peter O'Toole. 'Yes, which isn't bad, is it? I was quite pleased about that. I only had one day filming with him and he was exactly what you want Peter O'Toole to be, the most extraordinary presence and full of ridiculous tales – he was glorious. I got a photo of us together and I still keep it on my fridge.'

For a show that some reviewers billed as a 'sizzling bonkfest', there wasn't much nudity in it. 'No, but there's lots of sex,' David told one journalist, not that he was embarrassed by any of the scenes he had to play. 'I've kind of got over it now. There was some quite raunchy stuff in *Blackpool*, I suppose, so you kind of think, well, they've seen it before. Both my parents will be fine about it. They've seen me do a lot worse – gay love scenes, running naked across the National Theatre stage in the buff … they're not High Church holy, they're worldly and really pretty liberal.'

In fact, he continues, 'They thought it was hilarious [the sight of him panting and thrusting amid corsets and flounces]. You're aware that the tabloid press have an expectation that this is the story, and

Mum and Dad have been badgered about that a lot – they get people knocking on the door, which bothers me much more than it bothers them. They're very, "Come in and have a cup of tea," and I'm like, "Don't do that!" But they don't have Mary Whitehouse-style moral views.'

All the same, like most actors, he was still somewhat mortified at the prospect of doing explicit love scenes, but as the action happened mainly under corsets, behind canopies and beneath skirts, it was more of a rompy than erotic affair. The worst part for him, he says, was a flashback sequence of remembered encounters, including quickies with elderly ladies. One of them was at least seventy years old, he remembers, 'but all she did was rip off my shirt. It was, "Hello, Cynthia, I'll be under your skirt, okay?" I felt sorry for them; it was easier for me. They were only there for the day to get orgasmic on cue.'

There was one sequence, he remembers, when he is seen 'at work' and you see about 'twenty different conquests very quickly, and of course, those poor actresses. One is getting wheeled on while the last one is leaving, and they've got their skirts round their ears, but I have to say, they were all game! All the same, it's not the pretending to have sex that is embarrassing, it's being unclothed, and with an actress who is hopefully in the same boat, and you're just getting on with it. Pretending to climax on screen is about the most embarrassing thing I've ever done. Well, it's private, let's be honest! So there's all these cameras and everyone else is watching you, and you go for it the best you can, but there's a sense [of relief] when they say cut!'

But overall, he continues: 'It's fast, furious, funny and crazy. I don't think it's a Casanova that people will expect. He's not a lounge lizard, a lothario or a lady's man, he's a livewire, a free spirit, and people become attracted to that. He's almost an innocent, a puppy dog with all this energy and fizz about him.'

One of the things he was surprised about, though, was seeing himself plastered all over hundreds of billboards in Britain. He remembers, 'There were two enormous poster campaigns. It's quite weird to see yourself. I tend to look away – not that anyone passing by the posters is checking to see if you're there. But it's quite fun as well. I was on a bus in Edinburgh when I saw the face of one of the cast, Nina Sosanya and her enormous cleavage, and thought, That's my head resting on it! I quickly sent a text to Nina and said: "We're fifteen feet tall in Edinburgh!"'

When the drama was shown on the American PBS channel, just over a year after it had been broadcast in Britain, Anita Hall, writing in *The New York Times*, warned viewers 'not to let the lighthearted Venetian bedroom-balcony-to-gondola chase scene at the beginning fool you.' It was not in her opinion, a rollicking series of casual sexual encounters and farcical bedroom-window escapes. But it did, she reported, have 'a lively pace, a warm spirit, a contagious sense of fun, some very pretty eighteenth-century European settings, and Peter O'Toole as the title character in his later years.'

Casanova was broadcast in the UK in March 2005, and went on to become one of the most-watched dramas on BBC3 of the year, with significant recognition at the BBC Drama awards ceremony. Two months before this David played the lead role of Jimmy Porter in Richard Baron's production of *Look Back in Anger* at the Royal Lyceum, Edinburgh.

The Edinburgh production of the John Osborne classic marked his welcome return to the Scottish stage. The play that had marked the end of drawing-room theatre when it was first performed in London in 1956, with Alan Bates in the part that David was now playing. Although the character of Porter was a typical working-class anti-hero of the 1950s, who rallied against an unjust world and vented his bitterness and irritability on his wife, David hoped that audiences would be able to see beyond the anti-establishment reputation, with which the work had been labelled over the years: 'It is theatre that has been hijacked by history because it did what it did, when it did it, in terms of changing the face of British theatre. Its place in history almost overshadows what a great piece of work it is; it's no more a period piece than *Macbeth* is. It's not about the 1950s – it's a love story, a desperate, twisted, sexual love story.'

Directed by Richard Baron, the critics in Edinburgh raved about the pace of the production. When dates were played in February at the Theatre Royal in Bath, this same pace generated a feeling of high-octane energy and cleverly found time for the characters to settle into the silences in between them. That energy, wrote *The Stage*, 'is all but psychotic when it comes to David Tennant's Jimmy. He is like a caged animal with the petulance of a child and articulacy of a natural orator. Yet he oozes sexuality in a way that justifies the whole strange ménage à trois with his wife Alison and fellow lodger Cliff. And makes Alison's friend Helena's later passion towards him inevitable.'

As the *Times Online* concluded, David 'was superbly supported by Anne-Marie Duff's pale, dignified Alison and Steven McNicoll's likable, but maddeningly ineffectual Cliff. The decline of Helen McCrory's Helena from sexy confidence to tremulous self-loathing was almost too raw to watch.'

It was one month after he finished working on *Look Back in Anger*, during the same month that *Casanova* aired in Britain, when the unexpected happened. As luck would have it – for David at least – Christopher Eccleston, the Ninth Doctor Who, announced he would not be returning for a second series. He was concerned about the dangers of being typecast as everyone's favourite Time Lord – and, according to that same year's National Television Awards, he was a 'very popular' Time Lord. In addition, it had always been his intention from the outset to do just one series. Unfortunately, it seemed the BBC had prematurely announced the reasons for his departure without his consent.

Although the BBC released a statement on March 30, 2005, ostensibly from Eccleston, saying that he had decided to leave the role after just one season because he didn't want to restrict his career to just being well known for one role, one week later, the BBC had to eat humble pie and admit that Eccleston's 'statement' was falsely attributed and released without his permission. The BBC admitted that they had broken an agreement made in January not to disclose publicly that he only intended to do one season. The statement was made only after journalists had started bombarding the BBC press office with questions of how, why and when.

Making matters worse, for the BBC, on 11 June, when

Eccleston was asked during a radio interview whether he had enjoyed working on *Doctor Who*, Eccleston responded by saying, 'Mixed, but that's a long story.' Indeed his leaving the show had become such big news that the stories continued to fill Britain's tabloid press for some weeks after.

Within a couple of weeks of the BBC announcing Eccleston's departure the Corporation confirmed that David, who had been at the top of their initial shortlist over Bill Nighy, Eddie Izzard and Alan Davies when Christopher Eccleston was ultimately chosen, would replace him and was to make his first, albeit brief, appearance in Eccleston's final episode, 'The Parting of the Ways', on 18 June 2005, for the regeneration scene. Finally, his childhood fantasy was to become a reality.

According to Russell T. Davies, 'He [David] came to mind straightaway when we had to find a new Doctor. We'd established we were both fans when we were working on *Casanova*, and when Christopher left he seemed the obvious choice. It's a very hard part to play because a lot of character work is based on the character's past and with a 900-year-old Time Lord, it's hard to find the normal baggage. And he's the centre of every scene so he has to have great charisma and invention. I think David brings to it a fantastic sense of humour – he can find a lightness in even the darkest of scenes, which is a very human thing – and that's quite rare for a leading man.'

Looking back to when he was first asked to play the part, David says, 'I just remember laughing an awful lot because it seemed so hilarious. Then in the days that followed I did have a few wobbles because it seemed such a specific thing to take on – any long series

Above left: Playing a manic depressive in *Takin' Over the Asylum*, a BAFTA award winning Scottish television drama series about a hospital radio station in a Glasgow psychiatric hospital.

Above right and below: As PC Simon 'Darwin' Brown in *Duck Patrol*, a comedy series about a River Police Station that was broadcast on ITV in 1998.

© *REX Features*

David Tennant the theatre star.

In Martin McDonagh's *The Pillowman*, November 2003 (*above left*) and alongside Kelly Reill in *Look Back in Anger*, February 2005 (*above right and below*).

At the 2005 BAFTA award ceremony alongside his *Blackpool* co-star Sarah Parish.

Above: Starring alongside Kate Ashfield in *Secret Smile*, an ITV drama serial based on the Nicci French book of the same name, December 2005.

© *REX Features*

Below left: At the 2005 House Festival with former girlfriend, and fellow actress, Sophia Myles.

Below right: Having a celebratory drink with Sophia Myles and television presenter Chris Evans at the *Otherwise Engaged After Party*, October 2005.

© *Getty Images*

Turning on the Christmas lights in Cardiff with Billie Piper, November 2005. © *REX Features*

David and Billie rehearsing scenes for *Doctor Who*.

Inset: Local kids watch David and Billie Piper filming scenes for the 'New Earth' episode of *Doctor Who* at Rhossilli Bay in south-west Wales.

David Tennant won eleven awards in 2006. Here he can be seen, alongside Billie Piper, holding the *TV Choice* and *TV Quick* award for Best Actor (*above left*) and at the National Television Awards where he won the award for Most Popular Actor (*above right*).

Below: With Catherine Tate, filming 'The Runaway Bride', the 2006 *Doctor Who* Christmas Special, in Cardiff city centre, July 2006.

David Tennant, Billie Piper, Camille Coduri and Noel Clarke, the stars of David's first *Doctor Who* series, grasping on to the National Television Award for Most Popular Drama, which *Doctor Who* won in 2006.

© REX Feature

turns into a certain type of thing and this comes with so many expectations. Then I just woke up one morning and thought, what on earth are you thinking of? Just do it! You're only the tenth bloke who's ever got to do this – you'd be kicking yourself for the rest of your life.'

All the same, David admitted, taking over from Eccleston was still a daunting prospect. 'He has done a fantastic job of reinventing the Doctor for a new generation and is a very tough act to follow.'

Despite the fact that he was only the tenth actor to take on the role on the small screen in little over 40 years, he was just as eager to explain that time was running out for too many other actors to enjoy the same opportunity: 'Time Lords can only have 13 bodies, but I'm sure when they get to that they can find some storyline where he falls in a vat of replenishing cream or something. But so many factors decide what happens next year – it's not entirely down to ... I mean, if the show suddenly gets only two hundred viewers and I'm the only thing that's changed, then you'll have Charlie Drake as the Eleventh Doctor before you know it!'

Interestingly enough, work on the first-ever series of *Doctor Who* began in March 1963. BBC producers at the time wanted to fill the Saturday evening slot between *Grandstand* and *Juke Box Jury* and thought a science fiction series would appeal to all age groups. The first episode was broadcast on 23 November and, thanks to power cuts and blanket coverage of the assassination of John F. Kennedy, went largely unnoticed. In fact, *Doctor Who* would not make its mark until the appearance of the Daleks in the third episode of the first series that was broadcast in December 1963.

William Hartnell was the original Doctor, accompanied by his granddaughter Susan Foreman, played by Carole Ann Ford, and two of her teachers, who had been sucked into the Tardis: Barbara Ford (played by Jacqueline Hill) and Ian Chesterton (William Russell). For the writers, the introduction of new companions was a useful device to explain concepts to viewers by making the rookie assistant ask questions, or to further the plot by ensuring they got themselves into trouble.

Although the rapid turnover of leading actors must have been somewhat embarrassing for the BBC, soon after it was announced that David had taken over the role, a newspaper ran a story claiming that Billie Piper (who played the Doctor's assistant, Rose Tyler) was also planning to leave after Series Two, which in the end turned out to be true, for fear of limiting her career. This is kind of interesting in itself, when you consider that Piper was reborn in the role and went on to become a massive star. She was applauded as one of Britain's brightest and most popular actresses, collecting numerous award-nominations and multi-million pound contracts since she joined *Doctor Who*. Quite amazingly, she was to dominate her chosen profession for the second time in her career.

In 1998, Piper was the youngest solo artist ever to have a number one single in Britain with 'Because We Want To', which she followed with two other number ones, a platinum-selling album, and as Britain's equivalent to Britney Spears, she was on the brink of conquering America. But at the height of her fame, she turned her back on it, only to shock fans by marrying Chris Evans (the one-time most popular presenter on radio and television) – and enjoying one of the longest – and allegedly booziest celebrity honeymoons on record before reinventing herself as one of Britain's hardest-working and acclaimed young actresses.

Unlike so many before her, and since, Billie successfully made the significant leap from teenybopper pop star to acclaimed actress in the public eye. But what was more astonishing, perhaps, was how she came out of her divorce to Evans as a dignified, warm and talented woman, which won her huge respect and admiration from fans, the press and her peers the world over.

Shocking the world once again, three years after the breakdown of her marriage to Evans, she went along with his wishes to get a quickie divorce because he wanted to marry his girlfriend of nine months, professional golfer, Natasha Shishmanian. To this day, Billie remains good friends with Evans (who has now returned to public life with his own show on BBC Radio 2), and unlike so many other divorced celebrities, Billie has never sought a single penny from him.

According to some, it was a great shame that Billie decided to jump the *Doctor Who* ship because by the time she departed the series, David had nothing but good things to say about her and how he had clearly enjoyed the dynamics of the relationship of the characters they were playing, which of course in turn started the gossip columnists to draw their own conclusions about a real-life relationship.

It probably didn't help matters when the pair attended the première of Ridley Scott's epic *Kingdom of Heaven*, soon after it had been announced that David was to be the new Doctor Who. Recalls Billie, 'I've never seen anything like it. David and I have been to millions of things together, but that night the paparazzi just went hysterical for him. And he was a real bugger because he grabbed hold of me and wouldn't let go of my hand, so I was thinking that's really going to confuse people! I think he just needed a bit of moral support because it was so mental. People put two and two together and made five, but we shared a flat together for years in Glasgow so we're best friends. He's like my brother so it was all a bit weird, although it was funny, too. I'm likely to get taken out when he doesn't have anyone else to go with – I'm his stand-by.'

Although she said she had shared a flat with David 'in Glasgow for years', according to David, the first time they met was on the set of *Doctor Who*. So one has to wonder whether the flat sharing quote was taken out of context, or even worse, whether it was nothing more than tabloid tittle-tattle to make things sound more exciting than they actually were.

All the same, David had no preconceptions: 'She's just perfect. She was so welcoming and easy to work with, and I was nervous about that, because it's nine months and a lot of stuff to do together and that relationship has really got to work, just from a getting-through-the-day point of view, never mind the acting side. I really think she is a brilliant actress, too – in every take she's got something new, she makes it look effortless.'

He was equally enthusiastic about the way in which Davies, since he first took over the programme, invested the characters with an emotional life previously unseen in the earlier series, so that in many ways *Doctor Who* becomes a love story: 'I mean, they're not shagging, but in every other way, they're a couple. Like John Steed and Emma Peel. Mind you, he is about 900 and she's 19, so it'd be a bit Michael Douglas and Catherine Zeta-Jones.'

Just before summer arrived, David had already filmed his first lines. When he arrived on set, only a skeleton crew remained. The last episode of Christopher Eccleston's *Doctor Who* had just been filmed and there was an end-of-term feeling to proceedings. As he recalls, 'There was hardly anyone there, and yet you're sensing the importance of the moment. My first line was, "Hello! New teeth, that's weird." It was very odd, saying my first line as the Doctor.'

For him, one of the most attractive aspects of the role was the regeneration process itself: 'The fantastic thing about the regeneration process is that every time the Doctor goes through it, he changes to an extent. So as an actor, you get to work on a blank canvas where you don't have to worry too much about what has gone before. It's interesting, because he's always going to be the moral egalitarian, humanitarian, slightly wild, slightly anarchic bloke that he's always been, but because he's getting older he's moving on. He's seen it all before, every alien creature with a superiority complex.'

As Russell T. Davies explained, 'the regeneration is a huge part of the programme's mythology and I'm delighted that new, young viewers can now have the complete *Doctor Who* experience, as they witness their hero change his face,' something that was never seen in the very early series.

Almost certainly, the serious fans of the programme, more commonly known as 'Whovians', thought to originate from the 'Doctor Who Fan Club of America', who formerly produced a newsletter entitled *The Whovian Times*, and who, like the *Star Trek* Trekkies, are complete fans in every sense of the word, were already wondering what sort of Doctor Who David might create. It was something that was discussed in the bible fan publication, the *Doctor Who Magazine* (*DWM*, for short).

Officially sanctioned by the BBC, the magazine began life as *Doctor Who Weekly* in 1979, published by the UK arm of Marvel Comics. The first issue's cover date was 17 October and had a cover price of just 12 pence, but because of the practice of forward dating magazine covers to provide greater longevity on the shelves, this date is actually a week later than the actual release date, 12 October.

The magazine moved from weekly to monthly publication with the issue published in September 1980. The cover price increased to 30 pence and the magazine simply became known as *Doctor Who* (the tagline *A Marvel Monthly* was not part of the name, but simply a description that appeared on many of Marvel UK's monthly titles at that point). The title changed to *Doctor Who Monthly* with issue number 61 and then, twenty issues later, in February 1984, it became known as *Doctor Who Magazine*.

By 1990 the magazine started appearing once every four weeks, or thirteen times a year. Despite the BBC discontinuing production of *Doctor Who* in 1989, the magazine continued to be published, providing new adventures in the form of comics. When the series was revived in 2005 with Christopher Eccleston taking the role of the Doctor and Billie Piper as his companion Rose Tyler, it provided a new generation of fans that the magazine continues, to this day, to attract.

THE DREAM COMES TRUE

Originally geared towards children, *DWM* has grown over the years into a more mature magazine that explores the behind-the-scenes aspects of the series. Due to its longevity, it is seen as a source of official and exclusive information, sharing a close relationship with the television production team and the BBC. In 2006, however, it lost its exclusivity when BBC Worldwide launched its own comic aimed at a younger audience, *Doctor Who Adventures*.

DWM is now published by Panini Comics, which purchased the title along with the rest of the Marvel UK catalogue in 1995. At this time Panini also began to digitally restore and reprint older *DWM* comics in trade paperback format. Eight volumes have been printed so far: two featuring the comic adventures of the Fourth Doctor; one with the adventures of the Fifth Doctor; one of a planned series of two episodes featuring the Sixth Doctor; and four focusing on the Eighth Doctor. In 2006 Panini also published a one-off magazine-format reprinting of the complete Ninth Doctor strips.

But whether they bought the magazine or not, for many who grew up during the 1970s, *Doctor Who* was a defining childhood experience, with jokes abounding about time spent hiding behind the sofa for fear of the Daleks, the mechanical villains infamous for their robotic pronunciation of the famous line, 'e-x-t-e-r-m-i-n-a-t-e'! It is precisely this generation of children who today form the vast majority of Whovians. They are often serious fans of the series and often collectors of associated merchandise and memorabilia. As Christopher Eccleston says, 'I've met a number of Whovians, real serious *Doctor Who* fans, and they've been so kind and generous to me and excited about the series ...'

No wonder, when you consider that one of the most momentous dates in a Whovian's diary was Saturday, March 26, 2005. That was the day that all Whovians tuned to BBC1 at 7 p.m. to capture a moment they had been eagerly waiting for 16 years for: the first episode of a new series. Russell T. Davies was clearly equally excited. That afternoon, he says, 'I went into town, shopping and pottering about. There was a buzz in the air. I felt like I was eight years old again. It was like, "Mum's dragged me to town, and I've got to get home because *Doctor Who's* going to be on". I'll never forget that feeling. As long as I live.'

And it was no wonder he was excited. When the *Doctor Who* end credits roll Davies is billed as writer and executive producer, but that, it seems, is an understatement. According to Richard Johnson, writing in the *Daily Telegraph* in March 2007, 'He has a say in everything, down to the colour of the Doctor's suit. After filming, he watches all the rushes – every single frame of them. He works across *Doctor Who*, *Torchwood* and *The Sarah Jane Adventures*, writing the key episodes. And when there's an edit, or a dub, Davies is there.'

Some weeks before David shot his very first scenes he wasn't entirely sure how he was going to handle the role except that he knew he would not be using his native accent, a fact that had already aroused heated debate in his homeland: 'There'll be a bit of a story behind my English accent – it's not that straightforward. But anyway, I'm used to doing English accents, but no, I don't feel any great nationalistic need to be Scottish. I am comfortable with my background. I don't understand why there's this thing that actors from a certain place have to speak with the accent of where they come from otherwise they're somehow being un-Scottish. That feels very "small nation" to me and I think Scotland's a much bigger nation than that.

'Besides,' he continued, 'I really enjoy doing accents. The only one I did have a bit of difficulty with was Birmingham, which I had to do for a radio play. Luckily, when I got to the studio Frank Skinner was there – which helped a lot! Accents and dialects are good because they give you a way of changing yourself externally which allows you to key into a kind of internal shift, this helps a lot with building a role.'

In addition, he was only too aware of the weight of responsibility that comes with playing the Doctor. He knew how passionately his audience felt about the series and how they would have huge expectations of any actor who took on the role. In the past, pressure such as this has led to moments of desperation and he admits that every job has its low point when the nerves come crashing in: 'That's a regular visitor. I end up thinking, this will have to be the last job I do because, obviously, I'm messing it up so badly. Everyone else on set always seems much more relaxed and confident than me. I think that it's part of the psychology of what you do; you get used to it. But when you're in the midst of it, it doesn't feel like a part of the process, it just feels horrible and desperate.'

The look of the Doctor was another aspect that he felt the need to get absolutely, bang-on correct. In fact, if rumours are to be believed, he apparently begged producers to base his style on that of British celebrity chef Jamie Oliver: 'I'd always wanted a long coat because you've kind of got to swish. Then Billie was on *Parky* the same week as Jamie Oliver, who was looking rather cool in a funky suit with trainers. And I rang Russell and said, "Are you watching this? Could we do this for the Doctor?"

'They had wanted me to wear a stompy pair of posh boots, but the trainers were the one thing I did go to the wall on. I wanted something that I'd enjoy wearing, an outfit that would look good and feel right. We also wanted something that was modern, without being specifically en vogue. I wasn't trying to create a *Times Style* article about it, but I'm glad people like it so much,' he laughed. 'I also wanted an outfit that wasn't too authoritarian so that's why I opted for a scruffier-styled suit. It's more what you'd expect to see a student sporting than a college professor. And inevitably the look is influenced by the sort of things I like wearing.'

Because he had been watching *Doctor Who* ever since he was three years old, along with just about everyone else of his generation who grew up in Britain, he admits: 'I had probably made a whole host of unconscious decisions about how I was going to do it, years before it was an actual possibility. But to be honest, when it actually happened, I didn't sit down and draw up a list of quirks that I wanted to fit in to my performance. As with any other part, you take your lead from the script and what that character says and does. Once that is filtered through your own perspective and experiences then hopefully it will be particular and unique. I was always aware of avoiding any kind of self-conscious eccentricity. The Doctor may be a 900-odd-year-old Time Lord from the other side of the galaxy, but he still has to be a believable character or the whole thing collapses.'

In the end, he predicted that 'viewers are going to see a slightly more no-nonsense Doctor and that is influenced by what Chris did with him. We are more aware that he's someone who fought a war, lost all his people and, because he's the last Time Lord, the last authority in the universe, he's less indulgent, more ruthless.'

Much the same as Roger Moore may have felt when he stepped into Sean Connery's shoes to play James Bond. He continues, 'Taking over a role from someone who's been very successful in it is daunting, and taking on a character that people have such fondness for, and such expectations of, can feel a little overwhelming but of course it's those very pressures that make it such an exciting job to take on.'

Not long before he had taken on the role of Doctor Who, David had, interestingly enough, been involved in another BBC cult television classic of British science fiction: the remake of Nigel Kneale's *The Quatermass Experiment*. It was originally transmitted live, in weekly, half-hour episodes over six weeks in 1953, and, quite unbelievably, became lost in the BBC archive. Although the original had been a six-part series, the new remake was intended to be abridged-down into a single Special and, like the original, it would be broadcast live as part of BBC4's *TV on Trial*, a season of programmes created to examine past television trends and productions.

Although scheduled in a two-hour slot, the production finished after an hour and forty minutes, under-running its allotted time, whereas most of the original episodes had overrun, which to a certain degree had been expected before the new version went out on-air. After timings had been made at the dress rehearsal, the increased pace was attributed to nothing more than the nervousness involved in a live performance.

Adapted from the original scripts by executive producer Richard Fell, the new broadcast was directed by Sam Miller. Kneale agreed to act as a consultant and Fell and the producer, Alison Willett, had several meetings with the writer at his London home to discuss the script. Although Miller controlled the production's artistic direction, experienced outside broadcast director Trevor Hampton assisted him in controlling the technical aspects of the live production, which was broadcast from the QinetiQ (ex-Ministry of Defence) Longcross Test Track site in Surrey. Structurally, the story was kept close to the original, though set in a slightly distorted version of the present day. The climax was moved from Westminster Abbey to the Tate Modern, as the latter was easier to replicate in studio and there was no visible monster.

Jason Flemyng was cast as Quatermass, with long-time Kneale admirer Mark Gatiss as Paterson, Andrew Tiernan as Carroon, Indira Varma as his wife Judith, David as Briscoe, Adrian Bower played Fullalove and Adrian Dunbar was Lomax – now a Ministry of Defence official rather than a policeman. Isla Blair was cast as Home Secretary Margaret Blaker, a combination of parts of Lomax's character and two officials from the original serial, and she brought to rehearsals a photograph of her husband Julian Glover on the set of the 1967 film version of *Quatermass and the Pit*. Blair stated that she was delighted to be joining 'the Quatermass club'.

Original 1953 cast member Moray Watson (who had played

Marsh, one of Quatermass's colleagues) visited the set during rehearsals. The 76-year-old was invited to make a cameo appearance in the live broadcast, but was not available that evening. It was during the rehearsals for *The Quatermass Experiment* that David was offered the role of the Tenth Doctor in *Doctor Who*. This casting did not become public knowledge until later in April 2005, but his fellow cast members and crew were aware of the speculation already surrounding their colleague. In the live broadcast Jason Flemyng changed *Quatermass*'s first line for David's Doctor Briscoe from 'Good to have you back, Gordon' to 'Good to have you back, Doctor' as a deliberate reference.

The production was the BBC's first live made-for-television drama broadcast in over 20 years. In fact, the broadcast suffered only a few errors, with some fluffed lines, several on- and off-camera stumbles, background sounds occasionally obscuring the dialogue and, at the end of the programme a cameraman and soundman appeared in the shot. As the final credits rolled, the cameras showed actors celebrating and congratulating each other – they had no idea that they were still on air. However, this could be interpreted as the characters celebrating their survival at the end of their ordeal. On two occasions near the middle of the broadcast a large, on-screen graphic was overlaid, advising viewers that a major news story – the death of Pope John Paul II – was being covered on BBC News 24.

Drawing an average audience of 482,000, *The Quatermass Experiment* became BBC4's second-highest-rated programme of all time behind *The Alan Clark Diaries*, which were shown in April in

2004. Writing in the *Guardian*, critic Nancy Banks-Smith was complimentary, but noted that 'there were minor bumps in this production. One actor dried ... Another made a crashing exit through piles of broken glass left by the monster ...The last scene is still gripping ... I always said Nigel Kneale was a prophet.' She also commented that, for David, 'This was a useful dummy run for ... *Doctor Who*, playing a doctor confronted with a man-eating vegetable.' Meanwhile, in *The Times*, Sarah Vine wrote that *The Quatermass Experiment*, 'despite not always succeeding dramatically, did however serve as a reminder of how a clever story, a good script and some decent acting can be just as effective as millions of pounds worth of special effects.'

According to another reviewer, Stephen Hulse of *Television Heaven*, 'the performances themselves naturally vary from the consistently excellent to the obviously poor. But this is an expected natural by-product of the live nature of the production and as such can in most instances be forgiven.' The performances Hulse liked most were David as Doctor Briscoe, who he believed displayed 'all the charisma and conviction that has made him a rapidly rising star to watch'. He went on to comment that: 'Andy Tiernan as the tragic Carroon makes a strong impression in a role that could have been little more than "Monster of the Week" in the hands of a less skilled performer. And Indira Bower as Judith Carroon, while undoubtedly talented, fares less well, failing to convey the deep emotional turmoil required from a woman whose already unstable marriage is placed under the ultimate strain by the horrifically tragic fate that has befallen her husband.'

But the standout performance, as far as Hulse was concerned, came from writer and *League of Gentlemen* star Mark Gatis as 'the abrasive and morally conflicted' John Paterson, who had turned in a performance that depicted everything from 'confrontational and angry to heroic'. In fact, so powerful and impressive was his performance, said the *TV Heaven* review, 'that it often feels as if a genuine chance was missed by not casting him in the all-important role of Professor Quatermass himself'. But, despite such observations, critical or otherwise, in the end *The Quatermass Experiment* (2005) was regarded on the whole as a huge success.

In between filming *The Quartermass Experiment* and preparing himself to fulfil his dream of playing the Doctor, David (who is one of those actors who likes to fill his schedule with work, work, work) also put his voice to *The Adventures of Luthor Arkwright* for an audio adaptation of Bryan Talbot's Eagle award-winning graphic novel. He enthusiastically took on the title role of a man who can travel between parallel worlds in his attempt to halt the advance of the domineering Disruptors. 'It's a brilliant concept,' he raved. 'This is an extraordinary idea of parallel realities, it's just a cracking story. There is a good sequel so I guess if the first one sells thousands of copies I guess they'll want to do the second one.'

But Luthor Arkwright was just one in a long line of recordings that he was putting his voice to. By this time, he had already taken part in the six-part *Dalek Empire III*, in which he was to do battle against the war machines from Skaro, and he had also given 'a delicious performance' as the slow-witted Daft Jamie in *Medical Purposes*, brought comedy to the Time Lords in *Doctor Who Abound:*

Exile and was 'superb' as the blustering Colonel Brimicombe-Wood in *Sympathy for the Devil* alongside David Warner and Nicholas Courtney.

It had all come about because his friend, Toby Longworth, best known as a voice actor for his work on several high profile science-fiction projects including *Star Wars Episode I: The Phantom Menace* and *The Hitchhikers Guide To The Galaxy,* had worked in a similar fashion for Big Finnish Productions and then ... 'He introduced me ... I did one of them and they've used me every now and again. The one that I did with David Warner I was particularly pleased with, because it was my doing to get him involved. I've done a whole series of *The Dalek Empire* and the sound mix was out of this world. It's great to listen to that back, makes you sound fantastic, like a proper hero.'

CHAPTER 6
PLAYING EVIL

'If I was going to live there I'd need to have some really
good pals that you could just go and hang out with and just
be normal.'

(David talking about living in LA – 1998)

A lmost 6 months into the 9-month production of the *Doctor Who*
Christmas Special and the 13 episodes that had to be
completed for Series Two, David's first, he must have been pleased
to be given a respite from the 12-hour working days and 11-day
fortnights to attend the world première for his latest venture on
the big screen at the Odeon in London's Leicester Square on 6
November 2005.

David was genuinely overwhelmed with the public turnout. His
appearance, albeit briefly, as baddie Barty Crouch Jnr, in the then-
latest Harry Potter adventure, *Harry Potter and the Goblet of Fire*, the
fourth film adaptation of J.K. Rowling's immensely popular 'Harry
Potter' novels, was well received.

A LIFE IN TIME AND SPACE

According to producer David Heyman, 'This is one of the most challenging of all the films, so we needed someone who could direct a dark and suspenseful thriller, drive exhilarating action sequences and yet at the same time, be intuitive and sensitive to the comic angst of being a teenager. You've only got to look at films as diverse as *Dance with a Stranger*, *Donnie Brasco* and *Four Weddings and a Funeral* to appreciate that there are very few directors as skilled and multi-talented as Mike Newell.'

Certainly, says Newell, 'For me, the essence of this story is a thriller. There are wonderful set pieces, from the excitement of the Triwizard Tournament to the humour and heartbreak of the Yule Ball, but driving the story is this marvellous thriller in which something truly evil is out to get Harry – and only he has the power to do something about it.'

The film, like the book, focused, on the most exhilarating and difficult times of Potter's life as he returns to Hogwarts School of Witchcraft and Wizardry for his fourth year of study. Beset by nightmares that leave his scar hurting more than usual, Harry is all too happy to escape his disturbing dreams by attending the Quidditch World Cup with his friends Ron Weasley and Hermione Granger.

But something sinister ignites the skies at the Quidditch campsite – the Dark Mark, the sign of the evil Lord Voldemort. It's conjured by his followers, the Death Eaters, who haven't dared to appear in public since Voldemort was last seen thirteen years ago – the night he murdered Harry's parents. Harry longs to get back inside the safe walls of Hogwarts School, where Professor

Dumbledore can protect him. But things are going to be a little different this year.

Dumbledore announces that Hogwarts will host the Triwizard Tournament, one of the most exciting and dangerous of the wizarding community's magical competitions. One champion will be selected from each of the three largest and most prestigious wizarding schools to compete in a series of life-threatening tasks in pursuit of winning the coveted Triwizard Cup. The Hogwarts students watch in awe as the elegant girls of the Beauxbatons Academy and the dark and brooding boys of Durmstrang Institute fill the Great Hall, breathlessly awaiting the selection of their champions.

Ministry of Magic official Barty Crouch and Professor Dumbledore preside over a candlelit ceremony fraught with anticipation as the enchanted Goblet of Fire selects one student from each school to compete. Amidst a hail of sparks and flames, the cup names Durmstrang's Quidditch superstar Victor Krum, followed by Beauxbatons' exquisite Fleur Delacour and finally, Hogwarts' popular all-around golden boy Cedric Diggory. But then, inexplicably, the Goblet spits out one final name: *Harry Potter*.

At just 14 years old, Harry is three years too young to enter the gruelling competition. He insists that he didn't put his name in the Goblet and that he really doesn't want to compete. But the Goblet's decision is binding, and compete he must. Suspicion and jealousy abound as muckraking journalist Rita Skeeter fans the flames of the Harry Potter backlash with her outrageous gossip columns. Even Ron begins to believe his 'fame seeking' friend somehow tricked the cup into selecting him.

A LIFE IN TIME AND SPACE

Suspecting that whoever did enter Harry's name in the Tournament deliberately wants to put him in grave danger, Dumbledore asks Alastor "Mad-Eye" Moody, the eccentric new Defence against the Dark Arts professor, to keep his highly perceptive and magical eye trained on the teenage wizard. Harry prepares for the challenging Triwizard tasks – evading a fire-breathing dragon, diving into the depths of a great lake and navigating a maze with a life of its own. But nothing is more daunting than the most terrifying challenge of them all – finding a date for the Yule Ball.

For Harry, dealing with dragons, merpeople and grindylows is a walk in the park compared to asking the lovely Cho Chang to the Yule Ball. And if Ron weren't so distracted, perhaps he would acknowledge a change in his feelings for Hermione.

Events take an ominous turn when someone is murdered on Hogwarts grounds. Scared and still haunted by dreams of Voldemort, Harry turns to Dumbledore. But even the venerable Headmaster admits that there are no longer any easy answers. As Harry and the other champions battle through their last task and the advancing tendrils of the ominous maze, someone or something is keeping a watchful eye. Victory is in sight, but as they edge closer to the Triwizard Cup, all is not as it seems – and Harry soon finds himself hurtling head-first toward an inevitable encounter with true evil …

David was playing Barty Crouch Jr, whose character in the film, interestingly enough, differs slightly from the character in the book. Although he would be sentenced for the same crime as in the book based on Igor Karkaroff's testimony, once caught, there is no doubt of his guilt or insanity. He has already been released from his father's control by the beginning of the story. After the Quidditch World Cup, Harry actually sees Barty create the Dark Mark, the symbol of Lord Voldemort and the Death Eaters, which looks like a skull with a snake coming out of the mouth in place of the tongue. As a spell it is cast by a Death Eater whenever he or she has murdered someone – but Harry does not know who he is.

Barty approaches Harry, but flees when his father and the elite unit of the Department of Magical Law Enforcement arrive. When he is unmasked, he does not reveal how he escaped, and there is no mention of him getting the Dementor's Kiss in which a Dementor (a soul-sucking fiend) latches its mouth onto a victim's and sucks out the person's soul. David's character in the film makes a great break from the book by actually stating Voldemort's name, rather than the preferred 'Dark Lord' title of Death Eaters.

'The scale of it was huge,' enthused David. 'And to be part of that enormous beast is very exciting. They work at a very different pace as they've got money and time to spend. They're filming three hours' worth in a year and we filmed three hours of *Casanova* in three weeks!' But doing Potter, he says, was enormously enjoyable: 'It's a huge, great monster of a film, but at the same time it felt like a very friendly, creative place to be. Mike Newell is a fantastic director. I have quite a small part, but he was attentive, clever and bright. It was a great experience to visit that world.'

Daniel Radcliffe, who has played Harry Potter in all the films, was just as enthusiastic. And he was thrilled that David played a part in one of the most entertaining and thrilling adventures of the series. In fact, he told *SFX*, the leading science, horror and fantasy magazine, 'I wish there was more of David Tennant in *Goblet of Fire*. He's only got a few scenes and he's brilliant in all of them. He's so absolutely, fantastically watchable.'

Equally compelling was his role in *Secret Smile*, ITV's two-part drama that was shown over two consecutive weeks. It was the month after *Harry Potter and the Goblet of Fire* opened at multiple screens across Britain and America, and was well on its way to becoming the third most successful Harry Potter film, ending up with a more-than-respectable gross of $896 million worldwide.

Filmed in May 2005, a few months before he started work on the *Doctor Who* Christmas Special, *Secret Smile* was adapted from the bestselling Nicci French novel about Miranda Cotton, played by *Shaun of the Dead's* Kate Ashfield, who lands herself with the ultimate Mr Wrong in the shape of Brendan Block, played by David. Just ten days into their relationship, Miranda gets home to find Brendan in her flat. He's read one of her old diaries, and he taunts her about the time when, aged eighteen, she secretly slept with sister Kerry's boyfriend.

'Miranda knows something's not quite right with him and decides to end it,' said Claire Goose, who played Miranda's sister, Kerry. 'She doesn't think anything of it, then a few weeks later she discovers that her sister Kerry is now going out with Brendan,' who soon worms his way into the family's affections. He proposes to Kerry and gets to the sisters' manic-depressive brother Troy, who stops seeing his therapist under Brendan's influence.

'Kerry's quite vulnerable,' Claire continues. 'She's always been in Miranda's shadow and Brendan gives her confidence, but she's a complete innocent. From the family's point of view, Brendan is charming, lovely and brilliant with Kerry. There's no reason to doubt him, even though he's totally manipulative.' Miranda's life starts to fall apart as her attempts to warn her family about Brendan fall on deaf years. And matters soon take a much more sinister turn, with devastating effects for Kerry and Miranda's family.

'Brendan is a dangerous complicated character, he's the kind of boyfriend you don't really want to have,' said David at the time. 'It was a fantastic challenge to play such a sinister and compelling part; I loved indulging my dark side for a while.' To film the thriller, David and co-star Ashfield were given ice-skating lessons for the scene where their characters meet. 'Fortunately, we didn't have to be great skaters – just so long as we could stand upright and propel ourselves along,' David laughs at the memory. 'Having acted with Kate before on a short film [*sweetnightgoodheart*] and a radio play [*Island*] made it easier to play the part, but it felt weird being so cruel to her, mentally and physically. Kate's such a likeable, gentle person that I felt a bit of a heel. In Brendan's mind everything makes sense and is justifiable – I don't think he thinks he's appalling at all.' Not that Kate saw much of David outside of their scenes together: 'Brendan's a very unlikeable character and David was brilliant at playing him. He'd come in and do his scenes, be really horrible and go away again. I didn't mind having that image of him – I let it wind me up.'

'In many ways,' said David, 'Block is an egomaniac who refuses to accept his girlfriend's ending their relationship. Instead of sloping off like any self-respecting rejected lover, Block returns with a vengeance, starts going out with his ex-girlfriend's sister and wreaks havoc on her family.' Despite playing the part brilliantly, he is happy to admit that he himself has no such villainous side: 'I think everyone understands what it feels like to be dumped. It's always a very intoxicating and irrational thing to be that obsessed with someone – I hope I dealt with it better than Brendan Block.'

What he liked most of all about his role in *Secret Smile* was how it vaguely resembled something out of Alfred Hitchcock and, as far as he was concerned, there was nothing better than the darkness of a classic Hitchcock movie such as *Marnie* or *The Birds*. This tempted some journalists to suggest what an ideal Norman Bates he might have made for the 1998 remake of Hitchcock's original *Psycho* (1960).

From the outset, most of the critics loved his latest work. 'Great cast, led by a menacing David Tennant,' began one review. 'Nicely shot, carefully directed to build up the suspense.' And in another, 'David Tennant was a convincing evil, stalking fantasist … plot-wise, *Secret Smile* grabbed you by the lapels and dragged you along,' shouted the *Guardian*. Indeed, it was, said most, the darkest performance of his career so far.

Although David said he felt grateful for his single status during the making of the drama and how it would have been a nightmare, had he himself been breaking up with someone while playing Brendan, he did become romantically involved with one of his co-stars, Keira Malik, during and after filming. Best-known at the time for her part in the BBC's daytime soap *Doctors*, interestingly enough, Keira would go on to co-star with Billie Piper in *The Secret Diary of a Call Girl*, which captured one of ITV2's biggest-ever audiences since the channel's debut in 1998, and the biggest audience since August 2006. During its time-slot, it also became the top multi-channel show and remains to this day, the highest-rated non-terrestrial commission of the year to date.

But it seems the couple were not ideally suited because four months after David met Keira on the set of *Secret Smile*, they went their separate ways. Apparently, he ended the relationship by saying that his schedule on *Doctor Who* meant that he didn't have enough time to spend with her. Not that he was to remain alone for long. Within a few weeks of breaking up with Keira, he was reported to be dating another actress, Sophia Myles, best known for playing Lady Penelope in 2004's *Thunderbirds*. Once again, they met on set, this time while filming the 'Girl In The Fireplace' episode for *Doctor Who*, in which Sophia made a guest appearance, starring as Madame de Pompadour.

Like David, Sophia had always dreamed of appearing in *Doctor Who*. It was something she had wanted to do ever since childhood, even though when it finally happened, the experience wasn't quite what she had hoped for: 'I used to watch it as a kid, so you can't say no to *Doctor Who*, it's such a privilege. When my agent called and said I'd been offered an episode, I thought, brilliant, I'll meet the Daleks. Instead I was in a corset in Versailles as the mistress of Louis XIV.' But she had another reason to be pleased. As the show is filmed at an undisclosed secret location in Wales, it meant that she could be near her elderly grandfather, who lived near Newport: 'I thought it would be great because having been out of the country I'd get to see granddad. We did a couple of days shooting then I went over to see him at his old-age pensioner's home. That was great and when we met, I said I'd come again to see him that Sunday, but he dropped dead the next day. It was kind of meant to be, really. It was so lovely that I got to see him and we had a good old chat – it was very special for me.'

Although she was delighted at the opportunity to become part of the *Doctor Who* legend, Sophia winces at the memory of her corset agony: 'It was really uncomfortable. In that period, people would never have worn those things for longer than a few hours at a time, but filming can go on for 16 hours so it takes its toll. But it looks great, so you suffer for your art, I suppose.'

And it wasn't the only time she had done so. When she filmed *Tristan & Isolde* in 2005 on location in Connemara, in the West of Ireland and in the Czech capital, Prague, she suffered ordeals of fire and water as she acted out the role of Isolde, a woman caught between her passion for Tristan and her duty to the man she's been forced to marry. Disaster struck when her hairpiece caught fire: 'I was talking to the director, Kevin Reynolds, at the end of the day. I sat down and suddenly heard people shouting what I thought was my name ... "Sophia! Sophia!" Then I realised they were saying, "It's a fire! It's a fire!" I leaned back and my three-quarter length wig had caught fire on a candle on a table behind me. The whole thing just went up in flames and my life literally flashed before me. But there was no time to dwell on it, we had to get on with the next shot.'

Another hairy moment came when she was forced to plunge into the bitterly cold Atlantic for a sequence shot in Connemara. Just recalling it still gives her the shivers: 'I'm terrified by the sea – I love swimming in a pool, but not in the sea – I suppose it's fear of the unknown. It was so cold and the worst thing is, you're sitting in your wet things on the beach, knowing you're going to have to get back in the water to shoot the scene again. And we did it about twenty-five times.'

It was immediately apparent that David and Sophia felt far more comfortable not talking about their relationship to the press – or for that matter, anyone else. They were intent on keeping their private lives exactly that. However, David wasn't quite so reticent on the subject of the *Doctor Who* Christmas Special 'The Christmas Invasion' about to be shown at 7 p.m. on BBC1 on Christmas Day 2005, ending what had been a truly fantastic whirlwind of a year. From being a relative unknown he had literally rocketed to becoming a household name, but it was his upcoming role as the Tenth Time Lord that would cement his place in showbiz history.

CHAPTER 7
GOODBYE, BILLIE ROSE

'You always strive to know you're doing it right but I think the day you imagine you're getting it right is the day you should leave almost immediately.'

(David talking about self-doubt – 2007)

Six months after the *Doctor Who* welcome dinner held at a Cardiff restaurant in David's honour, he and his former co-star Billie Piper were still great mates. Meeting the press at the Wales Millennium Centre (where much of the series is filmed) to promote the second season of *Doctor Who*, just days before the end of the marathon 9-month filming block, they were demob happy as they looked forward to getting back to their normal lives. But as Billie wasn't intending to return for another series, clearly they would miss each other when shooting for Series Three resumed the following year.

'We've had a really good laugh,' chuckled David. 'But it's very difficult. Her flatulence is a big problem.' 'Yes,' Billie agrees, 'it really is! Fortunately we get along, and we need to because it's long months, it's quite intense and we're shooting 13-hour days. I feel like I've made a friend for life.'

At the time of the press call, only two episodes of the new season plus the Christmas Special had been shown. Even though David had only been on-screen for less than three hours, already he had shaken off the feeling of being the new guy. It seemed *Doctor Who* was now his show and no longer Christopher Eccleston's. With three well-received appearances as the Doctor behind him, it was as if he had been in the role for years.

Coming in for the first day of filming in July 2005 for 'The Christmas Invasion', was, according to David, the worst bit. Already he had dealt with all the hoo-ha that goes with the show and the fact that everyone is still so fascinated by the phenomenon that is *Doctor Who*: 'Obviously that partly makes it the most wonderful job in the world, but it also makes it the most terrifying job in the world. When I finished my first day of filming I remember going home to collapse because of the amount of nervous energy that had been building up in the months previous to getting going. I suppose it could have been awful, but I've been so welcomed by this extraordinary crew.'

And if he had any concerns about how he would be received by the public, he needn't have worried. He received the thumbs-up from around 10 million viewers for his debut turn at Christmas. And of course, back home in Paisley, his proud mum and dad were equally thrilled: 'They're West of Scotland Presbyterian parents, so they tell everyone else what they think I don't hear! They actually came down and visited the set. We had a read-through for episode two and a couple of the actors couldn't make it. Because it's set in Scotland they were delighted to be asked to read in. My Mum played Lady Isobel and my Dad played Captain Reynolds and they were in seventh heaven. They were genuinely cheesed-off when they didn't get asked to play the parts for real!'

Most of the filming of the Christmas Day Special was put together over the course of 10 uncharacteristically hot summer days in Cardiff, as well as an industrial park in West London, where the artificial film snow was dropped on and around the Tardis, and the killer Christmas trees and scary Santas threatened to steal the show. Much of the focus, however, was on David as the new Doctor. Naturally, everyone wanted to know exactly what he would be like.

As far as executive producer Julie Gardner was concerned, 'He's a more verbal Doctor – he's quite chaotic, very energetic, there are flashes of darkness to the character, and there's a lot of lulling the audience into thinking he's a kind of lovely, kind of interesting, fascinating character and then you actually see what the moral line is.'

David was in agreement: 'He has to be a good guy, he has to be heroic, he has to be morally impregnable and beyond that it's a kind of evolving thing, but ultimately the script is the thing that you've got to go on. If I suddenly decided I wanted to play it with a limp and the script has me running up and down corridors, then that's not going to work.' But perhaps the *News of the World* summed it up best when they described him as being 'potentially the most charismatic Doctor Who ever.'

But more than that, 'The Christmas Invasion' was quite easily guaranteed a significant place in the *Doctor Who* history books by virtue of being David's first full-length episode following his brief appearance during the regeneration process in the 'Parting of the Ways' episode. It was also only the second story that could charitably be deemed a Christmas Special within the normal run of *Doctor Who*. What is perhaps most interesting of all, though, is how well it worked as an entertaining story in its own right by picking up and developing the storylines of the earlier series.

Christmas Specials of any series can be notoriously bad and in many cases are frequently considered the low point of any television series, usually involving trite and saccharine messages about the spirit of Christmas or pantomime-like romps, but 'The Christmas Invasion' avoided such traps. If anything, it proved to be a refreshing antidote to the usual seasonal low points. For example, the idea of having snow in the programme, (which turns out not to be snow at all, but ash from the destroyed Sycorax alien spaceship) took it over and above all the usual run-of-the-mill Christmas Specials being aired on the same night.

'The Christmas Invasion' was essentially Rose Tyler's story. It is Christmas on Earth and Rose's mum Jackie is decorating for Christmas. Jackie's boyfriend, Mickey, is working at the garage when he hears the sound of the Tardis materialising, as does Jackie. They run outside and see the Tardis crashing through the sky only to hit various buildings. The new Doctor steps out and then he collapses, and he is quickly followed by Rose who explains how she saw him regenerate.

In a bid to boost Rose's spirits, Mickey suggests a spot of Christmas shopping. A good plan until they find themselves under attack from a sinister brass band of masked Santas. However, they are not the only ones with problems. Prime Minister Harriet Jones has just been informed that a British space probe, on its way to Mars for a Christmas Day landing, has gone missing. It has been kidnapped by a monstrous race intent on taking over the world known as the Sycorax who, to all intents and purposes, are skinless humanoids wearing mantles of bone, usually keeping their features concealed under helmets. On top of that, they are proficient in the use of weapons like swords and whips, the latter delivering an energy discharge that disintegrates the flesh of its target.

Meanwhile, back at the Tylers, Mickey and Jackie are trying to fend off a killer Christmas tree, while Rose tries to wake the Doctor. As David explains, 'It's a very difficult time for Rose. He hadn't prepared her for the changes he'd undergo. So whilst the Doctor is recuperating, Rose is trying to fathom out how she can save the world; she's also trying to understand how she feels about him now.'

He continues, 'They've got to rediscover each other and decipher whether they still feel the same about one another. Despite the new face, he is fundamentally the same bloke – he's still the Doctor and still has a huge amount of affection for her. However, it's not just the way he looks or the way he talks that is different: the Doctor's outlook on life has changed, as has the way he tackles situations. I think he's just hoping Rose can accept the changes and they can pick up where they left off.'

Indeed, at the start of the Christmas Special, agrees Billie, 'Rose feels so unloved and isolated. She's returned home to her mother and Mickey who, as ever, are there for her, but she feels like she's lost her best friend. The Earth is being invaded and Rose has no control over the situation. The Doctor, who is still going through the regeneration process, isn't there to give her the answers and she's scared.'

But, according to the pre-show press release, Rose had every right to be scared. Aside from being chased by killer Santas, she also has to help Mickey and Jackie ward off a killer spinning Christmas tree. Even though such scenes were incorporated to give viewers two essential elements of the festive season, as might be expected, there were perhaps much darker and more sinister tones than children were used to at Christmas, but then again, wasn't that the whole point of watching *Doctor Who*? If there were any objections or criticisms that younger viewers would be left terrified by the thought of Christmas, Billie didn't think that was anything to worry about.

She stated confidently, 'Kids love being scared. It's something I've learned since starting on *Doctor Who*. As adults we worry that kids can't cope with anything scary and that everything should be censored, but that is nonsense. Children are so inquisitive and I'm sure will be asking themselves questions such as "What if the tree came to life?" It excites them. Part of the series' success is that it challenges the viewers' imaginations, including the kids.'

David agreed: 'Being scared and having nightmares is part of our childhood. The Christmas episode does have some scary moments.

Sinister Santas, a spinning killer Christmas tree, and of course the Sycorax, but that's great. I don't think we should shy away from it – kids love fear.'

Another concern that the viewers shared would have been in keeping with Rose's own: that she might not be able to save the world single-handedly, but she was certainly prepared to give it a try. She hopes she'll come up with a solution, or at the very least, give the Doctor enough time to return. 'Rose is very smart,' says Billie. 'She's very instinctive and has great strength of character. She's travelled all over the galaxy with the Doctor and taken note of how he handles situations so she tries to mimic his actions.' But she laughs, 'It's very amusing to see Rose trying to copy the Doctor, but she looks up to him – he's her best friend, her personal hero and she believes in him, so she tries to act like him.' While Rose, Mickey and Jackie simultaneously try to find ways to save the world and revive the Doctor, Rose is also battling with the fear that when he eventually returns, the Doctor may not want her any more: 'Rose is so scared he won't want her to travel with him anymore. She has spent so much time with him, experiencing new and exciting worlds, that she can't bear the thought that this could be the end and the thought of going back to reality, working in a shop, fills her with dread.'

The Christmas Special was, in many ways, the perfect introduction to the new series, the first episode of which was aired a little over three months later and titled 'New Earth'. It was set early in the 5,000,000th century and saw the Doctor and Rose arriving at the new home of the human race following the destruction of Planet Earth. Zoë Wanamaker, who appeared in the previous series, was brought back as villainess-in-chief Lady Cassandra. Russell T. Davies was in the writer's chair, and with some new twists and turns assured, such as Cassandra inhabiting Rose's body, it was all in all, a superb start to the series. But everyone was still watching to see how David measured up as the new Doctor and even more so how he would interact with Billie as his assistant Rose, especially after the Doctor had spent most of the Christmas episode in bed, recovering from the regeneration process and therefore, there had been no real interaction between the pair thus far.

What quickly became clear was that this wasn't just a different leading man at the Tardis controls. Billie's character appeared subtly different as well. Fans said the new Rose came over as being more confident, less terrified of monsters and the situations she encounters and seemed far more at ease in the new Doctor's company. The vital dynamic between the two leads was there from the start. David's deadpan way of delivering a line was one factor that worked better than anyone could have expected. The production and editing staff on the set loved it. When they examined the footage and prepared to turn it into a broadcast-quality show, it was obvious they had a sure-fire hit on their hands. Onscreen and off, David and Billie had the perfect chemistry, one made in television heaven, and none more so than when they shared their first on-screen kiss together in the initial episode. Billie loved it. She said that it took three attempts to get it right and much of that, she joked, was down to the fact that they had both been eating egg and cress sandwiches, so 'we didn't do tongues', she laughs.

David said much the same when he was interviewed by Virgin Radio's Christian O'Connell, adding that Billie 'has a marvellous set of lips on her – she's got a great pout and it's all her own work.' But, of course, by the time they filmed the much-discussed kiss, it seemed David had made another impression on the young actress. 'She was calling me "David Ten-inch" as the months went on, but you'll have to ask her about that,' he teasingly boasted. But Billie just found it all highly amusing.

Any hint of a Doctor-Rose romance, however, quickly went off the boil in subsequent episodes, which many said gave Billie the ideal opportunity to prove her worth as an actress. As if to prove the point, there was enormous poignancy in the episodes that followed. The first evidence came in 'School Reunion', in which the Doctor first reacquainted himself with a lonely, yet dignified former assistant Sarah Jane Smith, played by Elisabeth Sladen, who originally portrayed the character in *Doctor Who* from 'The Time Warrior' in December 1973 to 'The Hand Of Fear' in October 1976.

She was loved not just by fans, but by an entire generation, enthuses Russell T. Davies. 'And she looks exactly the same. It's a shock to see her, you can't help being taken aback. But that really works on screen because you want that visceral shock of people saying, "Oh my God, it's her!" which is fantastic. It's that whole thing of bringing more emotional weight to the series for Rose to start worrying about what happens to the women who are left behind. Plus there's a robot dog! The scenes with K-9 are really joyful and funny and daft. There's a genuine daftness, a joyful eccentricity about *Doctor Who* that no other programme can do.'

In character, clearly, Sarah Jane loved the Doctor from the moment she met him more than a quarter of a century ago. In their travels, Sarah encountered the dreaded Daleks and their creator Davros, fought the terrible Cybermen, confronted the mad Time Lord Morbius and defeated the evil god Sutekh. She was even witness to the Doctor's regeneration from his third incarnation into his fourth. But all good things must end, and eventually the Doctor was forced to leave Sarah behind on Earth. She thought he had forgotten her after that, remembering her only long enough to send a robot dog named K-9 as a Christmas present. But when viewers met her again in 2005, Sarah Jane, still as intrepid a reporter as ever, aided the Doctor and his companion Rose against the alien Krillitanes, and her thirst for adventure was instantly reinvigorated.

Watching Billie in the part of Rose dealing with the unexpected rival made for a surprisingly moving episode and her emotions took full reign again, just one week later in 'The Girl in the Fireplace' episode. This time the Doctor really did fall in love with Madame de Pompadour, played by Sophia Myles, both on- and off-set.

Sophia was just one of the guest stars more than enthusiastic about playing a part in the series. Others in the line-up were equally impressive. They included Maureen Lipman, Pauline Collins, Peter Kay, *Little Britain* star Anthony Head, and of course, there was the return of Zoë Wanamaker from Series One, with one-time James Bond contender, Christopher Eccleston. Apart from the wonderful guest stars popping up on the cast lists, it seemed that the storylines created by Russell T. Davies were also helping to make waves and headlines for the show.

It wasn't long before *Doctor Who* fever was in full swing. The *Radio Times* produced a special fold-out cover for the edition that reviewed the series, with copies quickly becoming collectors' items often sold for many times the original cover price on auction websites such as eBay. Indeed, when the first episode, 'New Earth', was broadcast on Saturday, 15 April 2006, some 8.6 million viewers tuned in. Although that was nearly 2 million less than the first episode of the previous series, it was no surprise, really, when you consider that the third Harry Potter film, *Harry Potter and the Prisoner of Azkaban* (2004), was making its first television outing on ITV on the same night.

Not that it mattered. What really mattered was whether the viewers liked what they had seen so far – and it seemed they did. As if to prove the point, the following week, the ratings shot up to 9.24 million tuning in to watch the far-darker 'Tooth And Claw', which had Pauline Collins playing Queen Victoria, with Rose desperately trying to use the phrase, 'We are not amused'. But surely the highlight had to be the werewolf changing form, from human to monster (in echoes of Michael Jackson's legendary *Thriller* video and John Landis's ground-breaking movie from 1981, *An American Werewolf in London*), with the beast racing after all the good guys. Viewers were so gripped that even *Doctor Who Confidential*, the behind-the-scenes programme on BBC3, beat audience records for its channel.

Having the Cybermen return in the fifth and sixth episodes and then again, alongside the Daleks in the twelfth and thirteenth episodes was another triumphant idea. Exactly 40 years after their first appearance in the show, the Cyberman were given what was described as a 'new futuristic-retro' look. Led by Roger Lloyd Pack (Trigger from *Only Fools and Horses*), they enjoyed a high-profile double and expectations were so high that Cardiff-born *Blue Peter* presenter, Gethin Jones, accepted a role as one of them even though he would be completely unidentifiable in his costume. Interestingly enough, the concept of the Daleks and the Cybermen both appearing on-screen was first proposed back in 1967, but was vetoed by Terry Nation, the creator of the Daleks. The episode is the first conflict between the two species in the history of the show.

The plot consisted mostly of the Daleks and Cybermen waging a global war with humanity caught in the crossfire. The Doctor, the Tyler family and Mickey Smith all fight for their lives, trying to reverse the situation. They are successful, but at an emotional cost to the Doctor and Rose as they are split apart in separate universes.

Despite the undoubted success, there was a sting in the tail. In June 2006, BBC Wales confirmed what the gossip columns had been insisting for months – that Billie was leaving the show at the end of Series Two. In a press release, the BBC said that Billie as Rose, the feisty young companion of both the Ninth and Tenth Doctors, 'will leave *Doctor Who* in a nail-biting Series Two finale. Over the past two years Rose has been on an adventure of a lifetime, travelling across the galaxy with the Doctor. She's visited far-off futuristic cities in the year five billion and beyond; landed on space stations, where she's been a contestant in a deadly version of "The Weakest Link"; travelled back in time and met Queen

Victoria, Charles Dickens, Madame de Pompadour and her dead father; she has battled against the Doctor's deadliest foes, the Daleks and Cybermen; taken on Slitheen, Sycorax and Krillitanes and survived the end of the world and the blitz.'

Even though the BBC successfully avoided the minor publicity débâcle that struck when Christopher Eccleston departed under what was seen as unstable circumstances, when Billie confirmed she was leaving, the split was amiable. Even better, the door was left open for her to potentially return to the series at a later stage. As *SFX Magazine* editor Dave Bradley told the BBC News website, even though there had been a lot of rumours regarding Piper's exit, no one should be alarmed that she could never come back: 'Even if she did meet a sticky end, the door would still be open for her to return. No-one ever stays dead in science-fiction.'

Many may have wondered why Billie would want to leave such a hit show when she herself was such a popular character in it – and indeed, is still regarded as the viewers' favourite assistant to the Doctor. Although they were somewhat baffled by her decision to quit, she had her reasons. Like Eccleston before her, she did not want to miss out on any of the other opportunities on offer to try new things and certainly, she would not want to end up in typecasting hell, forever remembered purely as the girl who played Doctor Who's assistant. Even though she admits that she had experienced the most incredible journey of her career thus far, it was time for her to move on to more diverse and challenging roles: 'I can confirm it comes to an end, for now at least, as Series Two climaxes. I am truly indebted to Russell T. Davies for giving me the chance to play Rose Tyler, and to all the *Doctor Who* fans, old and new, who have been so supportive of me in this amazing role. Thank you so much.'

Davies was grateful she had helped give the show renewed popularity when it returned to the screen after a gap of some 17 years: 'It has been a wonderful experience working with Billie. We will miss her, and we wish her all the success in the world for her future. However, the *Doctor Who* team have had a whole year to plan this final scene and have created a stunning exit for her.'

Interestingly enough, since she first took on the role of Rose in *Doctor Who*, Billie Piper has received both critical and popular acclaim. She was awarded The National Television Award for 'Most Popular Actress' in 2005 and *The South Bank Show*'s 'Breakthrough Award for Rising British Talent'. As far as the BAFTAs went, however, it had been decided some time before the awards ceremony took place in the ballroom of London's Grosvenor House Hotel in May 2006 that if *Doctor Who* won any of the big awards, Billie should collect them on behalf of the programme.

As it happened, and perhaps almost to be expected, *Doctor Who* was a popular winner of the viewer-voted 'Pioneer Audience Award' and the BAFTA 'Best Drama Serial'. And Billie was a hugely popular person to be welcomed on to the stage. After kissing David, who was kitted out in a kilt and was seated to her left on the *Doctor Who* table, Billie wound her way to the podium amid uninterrupted applause. 'This is such a treat. Thank you. Thank you so much,' she told the audience. Back at her table, she and her colleagues were thrilled.

What was perhaps interesting about her departure from the show at that time was that it had been rumoured she would leave after the completion of the very first series. The British media regularly released conflicting reports about how long Billie would stay. In March 2006, she claimed she would continue on *Doctor Who* into its third season in 2007, but then on 10 May 2006, she was reported to be considering whether to quit the series, although she did express an interest in playing a female version of the Doctor in a future *Doctor Who* spin-off series that would have followed Rose's life after she left the Doctor. The idea was later dropped, which in itself said a great deal about her popularity in the show. On 15 June 2006, however, the BBC announced that she was to depart in the final episode of the second series, 'Doomsday'. Apparently her decision to leave had been taken a year previously, but had somehow remained a secret.

But of course, Rose doesn't actually die, but gets transplanted to the parallel universe where she's to stay with Mickey, Jackie and the alternate universe version of her father. According to a once 'confidential script not-for-circulating', that Billie Piper included in her autobiography *Growing Pains*, the story would begin with Rose's voiceover, which gave viewers an indication of what to expect: 'Planet Earth. This is where I was born. And this is where I died. For the first nineteen years of my life, nothing happened, nothing at all. Not ever. And then I met a man called the Doctor – a man who could change his face. And he took me away from home, in his magical machine; he showed me the whole of time and space. I thought it would never end.'

Even so, and although she gets to rejoin her family and friends,

Rose loses the Doctor forever. The fissure between the two parallel universes is closed, thanks to the efforts of the time-travelling duo (and conveniently solves the matter of the invading Dalek and Cybermen forces by sucking them into the void), but in the process, Rose is rescued by her alternate universe father and transported to that version of Earth just as the fissures are closed for good. With no way to travel back and her body missing on our version of Earth, she is declared dead on our Earth. This leads to the extremely moving final scene, where the Doctor finds a way to communicate with Rose by burning up a star and projecting himself on a beach somewhere in Norway. She somehow manages to track him down and they have only a few minutes to speak. Before the Doctor can confess to a crying Rose that he loves her, the communications link is broken. It's extremely heartfelt and viewers really couldn't ask for a better way to say goodbye.

The scene was filmed on 16 January 2006, at Southerndown Beach, South-East Wales, and was, as one might expect, rather emotional to the point that there were several tears on set. To help matters, David and Billie were not given their scripts for the departure scene until the last possible second. As David recalls, it was all very moving: 'It meant that Billie was leaving the show (although it wasn't the final scene she shot), and that was very sad because she is a great actor and had become a great friend. It's also a beautifully written scene, and even when we ran through the lines together on the make-up bus that morning we started sniffling. In fact, in the video diaries on the DVD you can see us both have a good old weep about the whole thing.'

GOODBYE, BILLIE ROSE

'Doomsday' became one of the most popular episodes of Series One and Series Two. *The Stage* commented that the Dalek-Cybermen conflict was the 'only thing worth watching' during the weekend it was broadcast on 8 July 2006, overshadowing even the World Cup Final between Italy and France. The parting scene was 'beautifully written and movingly played, with not a dry eye in the universe'.

Dek Hogan of *Digital Spy* agreed. The episode was, he noted, 'beautifully balanced and with moments of high excitement and touching poignancy,' but he criticised Catherine Tate's appearance as being unnecessary to end the episode and for 'breaking the mood' even though in some quarters it was regarded as essential for the lead into the then upcoming Christmas Special, 'The Runaway Bride'.

Stephen Brook of the *Guardian* was another who raved about the final episode: 'It was a high point of the modern series, highly emotional, scary and genuinely exciting.' He went on to state that Rose's departure was 'brilliantly handled' and compared positively the plot of a war between 'the greatest monsters in the programme's history' with the film *Alien vs. Predator* (2004).

CHAPTER 8
IDENTITY CRISIS

'I don't talk about my private life – I choose to define my own boundaries and not take every available publicity opportunity.'

(David talking about fame – 2007)

During a day off from filming Series Two of *Doctor Who*, and while not being allowed to shave off his sideburns by order of the BBC, David filmed a cameo role as star witness Richard Hoggart for *The Chatterley Affair* that would be broadcast the following March (2006) on BBC4. In a *Times Online* article, Hoggart's real-life son, Paul, who was just eight years old at the time of the trial, recounted the filming at a disused law court in Kingston, Surrey, where he watched David play his father in 1960, during one of the most notorious obscenity trials of the twentieth-century.

As Paul remembers it, 'David was in a small crowd of actors playing lawyers and members of the public, all in perfectly reproduced 1960 attire. Using archive videos, he had been practising my father's accent and intonation and captured them

121

rather well. He was wearing long Teddy-boy sideburns, which my father never had. Even so, it was all rather spooky. We were on location for a new drama by Andrew Davies about the *Lady Chatterley's Lover* trial, the celebrated test case for Roy Jenkins' 1959 Obscene Publications Act. Davies has mixed the genuine court transcripts with a fictional drama about two jurors engagingly played by Louise Delamere and Rafe Spall, who have a passionate affair inspired by the book.'

The trial has passed into history as a key moment in the rise of the permissive society immortalised in that famous Philip Larkin couplet. A closing caption in the film describes it as 'the first breach in the repressive dam of Establishment hypocrisy'. Others would call it the opening of Pandora's Box.

'My father,' continues Paul, 'was a witness for the defence. He had been called because the founder of Penguin Books, Allen Lane, had taken a shine to him after reading *The Uses of Literacy*, his 1957 book on working-class life and culture, and added him to his collection of unofficial consultants. It helped that he was then a senior lecturer in English at Leicester University and an ardent admirer of D. H. Lawrence. The defence had more than 50 "expert witnesses" on call, including the Bishop of Woolwich, E. M. Forster, Norman St John Stevas, Helen Gardner, Cecil Day-Lewis, Raymond Williams, Noel Annan ... But according to Davies, my father became "the star witness". That is certainly part of the trial folklore, mainly because his testimony was so startling.

'The prosecuting counsel Mervyn Griffith-Jones had been hammering away at Lawrence's insistent and repetitive use of "four-letter words". He read out long strings of them, struggling with the Nottinghamshire dialect, with unintentionally comic effect. My father asserted that Lawrence wanted to return these words, all commonly misused, to their proper, non-abusive meanings. He was probably right about Lawrence, though this project to purify the language cannot be counted a huge success. My father never used them at home either and I'd bet that he and Mum never used them in their intimate moments.

'The real showstopper, though, was Dad's assertion that the book was "puritanical", even the graphic descriptions of sex, because the whole morality of the book belonged to the English Puritan tradition of truth to one's conscience. According to Griffith-Jones's son Robin, the lawyer had been given a whole series of these cases and was thoroughly fed up with them but this was a new one. He was incredulous (Pip Torrens, who plays him, should get a BAFTA for his reaction shots) and counter-attacked with mounting scorn. Dad now says that he knew immediately that he had gone too far, but was determined not to give an inch. Previous witnesses, says Davies, "had rather tied themselves in knots" under cross-examination. Dad was a defiant working-class-lad-made-good, who, I am sure, rose to the theatricality of the moment. He was damned if he was going to be bullied by a supercilious barrister and he stuck to his guns unwaveringly.

'I can't believe Dad's evidence tipped the trial, as is sometimes claimed. In his opening statement Griffith-Jones had already famously asked the jurors (including three women) to consider whether this was "a book that you would wish your wife or your servants to read". According to Robin, he felt as soon as he sat down that this uncharacteristic bit of improvisation could have blown his case. Apparently ten jurors were disposed to acquit before the trial started, anyway. But their exchanges made great copy for the Chatterley-obsessed media. In Davies's drama, all these deliberations provoke lively discussions among the jurors.

'The introduction to the drama of the affair could easily have been naff, especially when the couple start to use the book as a rather preachy sort of *Lovers' Guide*. In fact, it is handled with great wit and sensitivity. Davies, then a teacher, recalls the era clearly – he was "a bit miffed" by the acquittal, having paid one of his sixth-formers about £5 to bring him an unexpurgated copy from Paris, which he could now get for 3s 6d (about the price of two pints). He uses the jurors' reactions to provide a subtle exploration of the ways in which attitudes to sex and authority were starting to shift.

'Davies says he was extremely nervous about his own sex scenes: "They are very raw and it is unusual to have characters talking about it while they are doing it." Griffith-Jones finished by reading out a passage with a thinly veiled description of anal intercourse, though without spelling this out. "He would have thought that very ill-mannered," says Robin. "Most people in the room, including my father, probably missed it." Not Davies's heroine Helena, though, who persuades Rafe Spall's Keith to try it. "You don't see a lot of that on television," Davies says. "I've just adapted Alan Hollinghurst's *In the Line of Beauty*, so it's been my buggery year, really."

'Inevitably, my own memories of the trial are sketchy. Someone stopped me in the street to say my Dad was in the paper talking about "that dirty book". My older brother Simon and sister Nicola made jokes about "Lady Luvverley's Chatter" and "Lady Chuvverley's Latter". Simon recalls some light teasing at school, mixed with sneaky admiration. I said I couldn't understand all the fuss about four-letter words. I used them all the time: "door", "coat", "road" … We were not told about the hate mail or the excrement in the post. Dad declined invitations to defend other books, such as *Last Exit to Brooklyn*. He said he didn't want to become a professional witness.

'In 1992 he wrote of his mixed feelings about the episode, given the sheer quantity of exploitative and degrading material then freely circulating. Had the price of artistic freedom been too high? Those doubts remain today, though he stands by his testimony about Lawrence's use of language and his English Puritan credentials. Perhaps the strangest effect of Davies's re-creation is that, despite everything, so many of the issues raised by the trial remain alive and unresolved today. "Was that OK?" asked David Tennant slightly nervously after he had done his turn as my father in court. "It was great," I said. "You did really well." And I meant it – about both of them.'

When the drama was released on DVD, in January 2007, the reviews couldn't have been better. Paul Mavis, writing for the online *DVD Talk*, called it 'an interesting look not only at an important historical event, but also at a sensuous, complex affair between compelling, thoughtful characters. Extremely well acted, written and directed, it is highly recommended viewing.' *Cinema Crazed* said much the same when they stated that it was utterly thought-provoking and quaint, while daring to challenge the audience's notion of depraved and or immoral: 'Are two people sleeping together in marriage more or less depraved than two people having an affair? Why? Does erotic fiction rot our minds, or does it just allow us to feel much more liberated and open in the sense of sexuality?

'Writer Davies manages to evoke so many questions and, for the observant audience, topics for debate about sex and society, while Hawes' direction presents a glossy atmosphere within the lives of the two jurors who find themselves seduced by the novel and end up in a tangled affair with one another in attempts to both liven up their own private lives and become as adventurous as the events in the book depict. It's a well done drama with the backdrop of moral debate and I was thrown by it. Fiction, both of the erotic and fantastic, unlocks our imaginations and whether it can be considered corruption is debatable.' In the end, they concluded, '*The Chatterley Affair* dares to raise that debate in an entertaining view of one of the most controversial novels of all time.'

Soon after filming his cameo and during another break from *Doctor Who*, David was cast in *Recovery*, a harrowing one-off drama for BBC1, about a man whose life changes after suffering a head injury. Written by Tony Marchant, the story centres on happy-go-lucky building firm boss Alan Hamilton, played by David, who sustains a serious blow to his head in a road accident. Overnight, he turns into a completely different person. He has irrational rages and cannot be left alone to perform simple tasks such as dressing himself or making a piece of toast. He has also lost the ability to empathise and becomes a stranger to his loving wife, played by Sarah Parish, and their two boys.

David told *TV Choice* that as part of his research for the role, he met people who suffered in the same way as Alan and was deeply affected by the experience: 'We met one chap who tried to tell us all the degrees he had. It was an extraordinary list, but he couldn't remember them all. It was very poignant to witness their frustration. The randomness of these accidents almost makes it worse.

'You can be very careful crossing the road, but you can't legislate for an accident that happens out of the blue. All the head injury victims we met were very keen that we didn't show Alan and Tricia living happily ever after — that sort of injury is so fundamental to who you are that you're not going to get back to where you were before. It would be insensitive and wrong to suggest that Alan and Tricia could slot straight back to their old life. As Tricia says in the story, "I want two children, not three." But she simply has to come to terms with the new reality. It's a tragic, tragic story.'

But, as David continues, 'Our brain is our personality — if that gets knocked sideways, you become fundamentally different. You can't imagine what it must be like to be married to someone who becomes a different human being.' And it is that which is at the centre of *Recovery*. David as Alan is a husband and father whose personality is all but wiped out after a traffic accident, and with Sarah Parish as Tricia, the wife who must find new ways of loving the stranger sitting in her living room, it is an unsparing portrait of a family crisis.

Says Tony Marchant: 'I was approached to write a play about memory loss. It was only when I started researching the effects of brain surgery that I realised how completely our identity is bound up with memory, how much of human relationships are based on the knowledge of shared history. And how difficult it is for a brain-injured person when that personal history disappears and you're trying to claw your way back to find out who you are.'

Throughout, he worked closely with the brain injury charity Headway and his tightly researched scenario pulls no punches. As most critics agreed, David's frustration sparks like static from the screen and Parish is equally impressive as the wife who meets the demands of caring for her husband – a physically healthy adult, who can now no longer make his own toast nor govern his sexual impulses – with a believable balance of heroism and human frailty. For both actors, meeting survivors of brain injury and their families was crucial to their understanding of the project.

'This is an incredibly sensitive subject,' David added. 'It would be fantastically disrespectful to turn up on the first day of the shoot and say, "Right then, brain injury, let's wing it." I read masses of case studies and personal testimonies, but by far the most important thing was meeting the people at the Headway facility in Essex and talking to men who have experienced what [my character] Alan goes through, but there came a point where I had to stop. I felt I was learning too much about it and it was important for me not to know what was going on, for everything to be as brand new and bewildering to me as it is to Alan.'

Sarah Parish, who at the time was well on the way to becoming a veteran three-time co-star of David's, (and had joked that in 20 years time they would probably be doing a ropey old sitcom in a terraced house in Preston) agreed: 'A lot of people we met were concerned that they should be represented correctly because brain injury is something no one really knows very much about. Maybe because they're embarrassed to ask, maybe because the person involved is embarrassed to tell them, so I think to tackle these things in a drama is great.'

According to Joanna Wright of Headway, lack of public awareness is one of the hardest things survivors of severe brain damage have to face: 'David's character looks absolutely fine, but he's got a lot of cognitive deficits resulting from his accident and people like him often face a great lack of tolerance over some of their issues.

'The fact that every brain injury is unique, depending on which part of the brain is damaged, makes promoting the difficulties faced by sufferers even harder. Cognitive deficits can include a lack of social and sexual inhibition, extreme emotional instability and problems with communication. Sufferers may know what they want to say, but can't get the words out, which of course cranks up the frustration even more,' she continues. 'It becomes very socially isolating because you've only got to yell at a friend a few times and people think, Well, I can't cope with that. Friends back away and family members often do the same. In many cases, marriages don't survive.

'Every single day when we were filming I had to ask myself, "What would I do in this woman's situation? Would I go or would I stay with a man who looks like my husband, but doesn't speak, or act or even feel like him?" It's a kind of bereavement, but a bereavement you can't get over – you're reminded of your loss every day because this person who isn't your husband is there in front of you. My character, Tricia, is fallible. She gets angry, she gets things wrong. I'm glad she wasn't written as some kind of angel at the bedside because I think the guilt and pressure put on women by society in these matters is heartbreaking.'

Marchant agrees: 'It's an almost impossible task for most people. Does a wife have a moral responsibility to stay with a character who has become impossible to live with, but through no fault of their own? To deal with the loss of sexual, romantic and intellectual sharing that a marriage is based on, as well as the practical implications of becoming a carer instead of a partner, you either have to be a saint or you have to learn to expect less from your life together because there's no miracle cure.

'*Recovery* is almost an ironic tale, because for sufferers of severe brain injury – and there are about 1,500 people a year, mainly young men, who go through the kind of thing Alan experiences – it's a lifelong condition. There comes a point, not in all cases, but in most, where you can't beat around the bush with that. It's something all the men at Headway said to me: "Don't have a bloody happy ending." On the other hand you're writing a drama, you have to offer some redemptive glimmer. And when love is affirmed in these extraordinary difficult circumstances, you're touching something profound and extremely moving.'

Perhaps it was not surprising that soon after completing the film, David became a patron of Headway: 'The families we worked with were so extremely generous in laying out the reality of their lives for us,' he said at the time. 'I hope we've done them proud. I know I've come away from the experience with a hugely increased sense of just how fragile we all are. I now really, *really* look when I'm crossing the road. For me, *Recovery* doesn't play like some big-issue-led campaigning piece, but it makes you think; it makes you grateful you're able to think.'

According to one review in the *Liverpool Echo*, 'David Tennant is such a fine actor that if he chose to read the phone book on prime-time telly I'd probably tune in to watch. Fortunately the current Doctor Who was served with an idea and a script so good – and co-stars to match – that his role of Alan Hamilton is perhaps the best thing he's ever done. In turn comic and tragic, his behaviour veers between anger and frustration at being unable to perform simple tasks such as getting dressed to vulnerable and child-like, as he slowly realises that the man he was may never come back. This could have been bleak viewing, but Tennant has a comic touch that managed to find the humour in the absurdity and sadness of a situation faced by more than 100,000 people every year. It was a tour de force performance, too, for Sarah Parish as wife Tricia struggling to come to terms with the fact that the man she loved may be gone forever. The power of the piece lay as much in her journey in learning to live with a near stranger as it did with Tennant's remarkable skill, inhabiting a role none of us would wish to experience in real life.'

And the review in the *Herald* echoed much the same sentiment: 'If you didn't watch *Recovery*, you just won't know that the play was one of TV's saddest, most harrowing dramas ever – and one that should, if there's any justice, produce bucket-loads of awards for its two stars: David Tennant and Sarah Parish. Jolly entertainment, *Recovery* wasn't; heart-breakingly educative, it was.'

Indeed, agreed the *Guardian*, 'There was nothing remotely funny about *Recovery*, Tony Marchant's moving drama about a family dealing with the aftermath of a horrible accident. It seems to be something a serious actor has to do – play someone with up-there problems. Hoffman's done it, DiCaprio… as have lots of other major movie stars I can't quite think of right now. Here, on a smaller scale, our own David Tennant (taking a break from the Tardis) is playing Alan, who's been left with severe brain damage after being run over. He's extremely good at it, totally convincing as the husk of his former self. And Sarah Parish is also brilliant as his broken wife. It wasn't over-sentimental, just believable. And much more powerful for that. Anyone who says they didn't have a lump in their throats is either an unfeeling brute or a liar.'

Since *Recovery* was such an outstanding drama, beautifully written, acted and filmed, it is somewhat surprising that it was totally overlooked in the plethora of awards shows to which both Hollywood and Britain now abound. Clearly a favourite with most critics, who might have expected it to gain at least a 'Best Actor' nomination for both its lead stars at the television BAFTAs, strangely it didn't even receive a mention.

CHAPTER 9

FROM CYBERMEN TO DALEKS

'They've been around since the '60s so they are a real iconic *Doctor Who* monster. After the Daleks they are probably *the Doctor Who* monster.'

(David talking about the Cybermen – 2006)

Five months after *Recovery* was screened in February 2006 on BBC1 and it had received such outstanding reviews from just about every critic in Great Britain, Freema Agyeman, a little-known actress from North London, was about to secure the most coveted role on television, and indeed of her career. Apart from the seemingly obligatory appearances in shows such as *The Bill*, *Casualty* and *Silent Witness*, her biggest role up until then had been as Lola Wise, a kitchen assistant in *Crossroads*, when it returned to British television screens in 2003. She was nominated for Best Newcomer in the British Soap Awards and for Sexiest Female in the *What's On TV* magazine awards that same year.

Now, three years later, in July 2006, she was about to be seen in a minor role in 'Army of Ghosts', Billie Piper's penultimate episode in *Doctor Who*, in which her character, Adeola, would meet a terrible fate at the hands of the Cybermen (who she still finds more frightening than the Daleks). Little did she know but her performance was being closely scrutinised by Russell T. Davies, whose first impression of the young actress was how good he thought she was, and how she would make a perfect replacement for Billie.

Even though the search for a new companion to replace Billie had been underway for some time, recalls Davies, who had, at one point had even considered Hollywood's new Bionic Woman and former *EastEnder*, Michelle Ryan, no one seemed to capture what he was looking for until he spotted Freema. 'Watching her during filming,' he said, 'confirmed what an exciting new talent she was, so we called her back in to audition with David for the role of the new companion. Her range, presence and charm blew us all away. David and Freema are terrific together and we're delighted to have chosen her to join the Doctor for more adventures in time and space. The first scripts have been written and Freema's brilliant addition to the Tardis crew [will be] the perfect foil for the Doctor.'

David was equally enthusiastic: 'Freema was a joy to work with in Episode 12 of the current series. She is not only very talented and very beautiful, she's great fun and I'm delighted she's coming on board the Tardis full-time. I can't wait to welcome her into the Who family.'

But, according to Freema, the process of winning the role wasn't quite so straightforward: 'I auditioned for two roles in the summer of 2005, and apparently I'd been earmarked from then. I've learned all this since – I had no idea at the time. Subsequently, I got one of the parts – Adeola from "Army of Ghosts" – but during filming I was introduced to executive producers and bigwigs. At the time, I didn't think there was anything strange about that. A few weeks later, my agent rang me and said the bosses were quite keen on auditioning me for a part in the *Doctor Who* spin-off, *Torchwood*.

'So I went for an audition in London,' she told *Doctor Who Magazine*. 'But I had to miss the second audition because I got sick for a week in January. It was really awful, I was so upset. But then they said that they'd reschedule it. And then, just before the third audition, I got a call from my agent. She said, "All this time, they've been seeing you for the part of the new companion in *Doctor Who*, not for a regular in *Torchwood*." I couldn't believe it.'

In all, she continues, 'I had two auditions and just before I was invited to a screen test, they called my agent and said it was actually for the Doctor's new companion. A day after, I was on my way to Cardiff on the train with the casting director to screen test with David Tennant in the producer's flat. I was so glad they didn't tell me any earlier than that – I didn't have time to get nervous.'

She did, however, when she signed up to the series, request an on-screen kiss with David. She was apparently so desperate to be a success in following in the footsteps of Billie's Rose Tyler, who herself had enjoyed a kiss with the Doctor, that she didn't want to be left out. 'I asked for a clause in my contract that ensured a screen kiss with him. Billie is a hard act to follow, but David couldn't have been more friendly.'

Just days before 'Doomsday', the final episode of Series Two (and Billie's final scene) was shown, the BBC announced Freema would be the Doctor's new assistant. For the young actress, it was a huge relief that the news was now out in the open. 'I've been keeping this secret from my friends for months – it's been driving me mad,' she said at the time. 'Auditioning with David in secret down in Cardiff was unbelievable, but never in my wildest dreams did I think that I'd actually become the new companion.'

With her skills in the martial arts department far greater than those of her predecessor, perhaps one of the ideas behind casting Freema as the new assistant was to introduce a more physical characteristic into the role as opposed to Billie's more empathetic and deductive approach. As Freema acknowledges, 'Change isn't always seen as a good thing, but fans surely appreciate that the common components of the show are that the Doctor regenerates and the companion changes.'

Although excited to become part of the unique history that is *Doctor Who* (her favourite Doctor was Sylvester McCoy, and Bonnie Langford and Sophie Aldred her favourite assistants), she was also very much aware of what she was taking on and the potential difficulty she would have to face in stepping into Billie Piper's shoes: 'Billie did an amazing job on *Doctor Who* and was totally taken into the hearts of the audience, rightly so. But in years to come, I didn't want to look back at my time on *Doctor Who* and think that I'd worried about possible comparisons. Ultimately, I don't feel pressured into replacing the character of Rose, just her role as a companion. I hope the fans are willing to go on new adventures with me. It still hasn't quite sunk in – I'm sure it will slam home first day on set when I'm stood gazing at David Tennant!'

According to Richard Simpson, writing in the *Daily Mail*, Freema – incidentally the first black assistant in the history of the programme – would earn an estimated £80,000 for her 13 episodes in Series Three, apparently only half as much as Billie Piper earned for each of the two series in which she appeared. And if she herself was excited, which she undoubtedly was, then her former neighbours from the Woodberry Down housing estate in Finsbury Park, North London, where she was born and grew up, were equally thrilled. According to one of them: 'She was a beautiful happy-go-lucky girl who lit up the estate. And that's quite an achievement considering what this estate is like [rundown, with dozens of derelict, boarded-up flats]. She was never hanging around in gangs like the others, but was as good as gold. Not a lot of people achieve what she has done from this estate and we are all delighted for her. She's a star.'

As viewers would discover in the episode 'Smith and Jones', at the start of Series Three and just over three months after the 2006 Christmas Special aired, Freema would be playing Martha Jones, a medical student, who is not that far off from qualifying as a doctor. While Rose seemed in awe of the Doctor, there would be something of a power struggle between him and the newcomer. As Freema explained, 'Martha has qualities similar to Rose, and that's what attracts the Doctor to her. She's brave, feisty and level-headed. He doesn't want a shrinking violet, after all.'

But, she continues, 'She's older than Rose, more secure, but she doesn't have a boyfriend. She has her own little flat and her family around her. Rose had only her mum, but Martha has a big family. She isn't looking to the Doctor for guidance or education, she wants adventure! She hasn't kissed her old life goodbye though, and I think she intends to go back to qualify as a doctor. There are funny moments when the Doctor says, "I'm the Doctor" and Martha says, "So am I!" She speaks her mind.'

Right up until the cameras started rolling, she was pinching herself as she tried to come to terms with the fact that she had landed such an amazing role. She couldn't wait to get started: 'It's been nerve-wracking but David has been brilliant in helping me to adjust on my first days on set. I am really looking forward to travelling through time and space with him over the next eight months.'

Russell T. Davies shared her enthusiasm: 'We were delighted and honoured by the second series' success and we can promise new thrills, new laughs and some terrifying new aliens. The Doctor and Martha are destined to meet William Shakespeare, blood-sucking alien Plasmavores, The Judoon – a clan of galactic stormtroopers and a sinister intelligence at work in 1930s New York.'

That 'sinister intelligence' was, of course, the Doctor's old adverse enemy, the Daleks. No sooner had the Tardis brought the Doctor and Martha to New York City in the early days of the Great Depression than they learnt of a rush of disappearances amongst a burgeoning 'Hooverville' transient community. With the help of Solomon, the Hooverville's unofficial mayor, the Doctor discovers a race of genetically-engineered Pig Men living in the sewers. Their masters are none other than the dreaded Daleks, who have perverted the construction of the Empire State Building in order to spearhead the next stage in their race's evolution.

As reviewer Mark Wright wrote in *The Stage*, 'with such a glorious title [as 'Daleks in Manhattan'], how could this episode of *Doctor Who* fail to hit all the right buttons, whether you're die-hard fan or mainstream viewer? It had everything, from a well-realised setting, Daleks trundling through corridors, showgirls, fantastically "Noo Yaark" accents, a lead actor who is at the top of his game and Pig Men.'

Having set Dalek stories in the future and in the present during previous outings for the new series, it wasn't really that surprising that Russell T. Davies came up with the idea to have the Doctor's favourite adversaries appear in the Earth's past. After all, it had worked a treat when previously attempted, most notably in the 1967 episode, 'The Evil of the Daleks', and of course, in the second of the Daleks big screen outings, in Gordon Flemyng's *Dalek's Invasion Earth 2150 AD* in 1966, which starred Peter Cushing as the Doctor. This time, though, Davies had pictured a two-episode adventure set in the depression of 1930s New York City, (which would certainly help set designers transform the Cardiff docks into a setting that represented their Gotham equivalents).

Davies also wanted to play up the Daleks' genetically-engineered nature, which he imagined would make them skilled in the discipline, and in turn, inspire their Pig Men servitors. The whole thing seemed to have recreated the feeling of the old Dalek episodes from the early days of the series when Daleks got on with being Daleks, and it ended up being very refreshing.

As Wright correctly pointed out in his review, 'there's nothing more iconic than the Doctor crouching down in a dingy corridor, watching as the lower part of a Dalek casing trundles past the camera – those moments possess a kind of race memory effect in any audience member over thirty-five that send a pleasurable shiver down the back of your spine.'

Equally superb, Wright said, was David himself. In his opinion he thought the departure of Billie Piper as Rose had unleashed him and allowed his performance to shine even more than it did before. The supporting cast were also brilliant, according to Wright. *Spooks* actress Miranda Raison, he said 'gave a startlingly different performance as the ditzy but resolutely brave Tallulah. She's beautifully caricatured yet thoroughly believable – if the Doctor is ever in need of a new companion, I'd suggest a return to New York to pick her up.' Overall, he concluded, it was old-school *Doctor Who*. 'Daleks in Manhattan', he said, 'evoked the classic black and white days of [William] Hartnell and [Patrick] Troughton with the breathless style and pace of new *Who*.'

Wright was not, however, so thrilled with the second part of the two part episode. 'Evolution of the Daleks', he said, was hugely disappointing even though he had found it as enjoyable as he possibly could. 'Everything lacks the focus and restraint displayed in "Daleks in Manhattan", and "Evolution" feels like a marathon runner sprinting for the finish line and not caring about how they look when they get there. And when you get to the finish line, it turns out not to be as great as you thought it was. When you have such big things in this episode – Daleks, New York, the Empire

State Building, to have your climax played out in the auditorium of a theatre seems like short change for the audience.'

But then again, as Wright correctly pointed out, *Doctor Who* was always at its best when the Daleks were around. The Daleks had their own unique history. Ever since the Doctor first encountered the Daleks in the episode, aptly named, 'The Daleks', in 1963, the year the show began, they have been an essential part of the programme. On their first appearance it became known they were the product of a nuclear war between the Dalek and Thal races on the planet Skaro, a war that the Daleks claimed in the second part of the episode had occurred over five hundred years ago and had left them more or less confined to their city, in which they could only move about from the static electricity conducted from metal walkways. By the end of the two-part serial the Daleks were seemingly wiped out, which at the time seemed a fitting conclusion because initially they were not intended to be a recurring adversary for the Doctor. But their popularity increased so much among viewers that a return seemed inevitable.

Indeed, they were back one year later, in the 1964 episode, 'The Dalek Invasion of Earth', which suggested the Daleks had conquered and occupied the Earth in the mid twenty-second century. The sight of the Daleks amid familiar landmarks around London made their presence doubly effective by bringing the threat to home ground, but the Doctor explained away their presence by saying the events were taking place a million years before the Daleks and that what they were witnessing was the middle period of Dalek history. However, as an invasion force these

Daleks were able to move without the need for metal paths, presumably drawing power through the use of what appeared to be radio dishes on their backs. The question why Daleks in the future would be more restricted than these particular Daleks was never explained and of course, the million years' answer is usually disregarded and contradicts the timeline given in 'The Daleks'.

Over the course of their next few appearances, the Daleks developed more and more ability for time travel, growing more and more powerful, and by comparison, further removed from the almost pathetic monsters of the first serial. The radio dishes also vanished and Daleks were able to move under their own power. Given the time travel nature of the series, whether these stories took place chronologically in the order in which they were transmitted is uncertain and debate continues to this day as to their proper sequence. The only given date is 4000AD for 'The Daleks Master Plan', though some presume that another episode, 'The Power of the Daleks', shown in 1966, took place before 'Dalek Invasion of Earth' as none of the human characters recognise the Daleks.

A second attempt to end the Dalek saga was made in 'The Evil of the Daleks' in 1967, which also introduced a Dalek Emperor. This time, the conflagration caused by a Dalek civil war was declared by the Second Doctor (played by Patrick Troughton) to be the final end. Much of this was down to the fact that Dalek creator, Terry Nation, was in negotiations to sell the Dalek concept to American television. Although the sale did not succeed, the Daleks remained unseen for the next five years, but they did return in the third *Doctor* serial, 'Day of the Daleks' (1972), when once again they used time-travel technology. The Daleks were re-established as a species bent on universal conquest, as seen in 1973's 'Frontier in Space' (which led directly to 'Planet of the Daleks') and later on to 'Death to the Daleks' in 1974. Apparently, the Dalek Emperor was not in attendance so they were led by a Supreme Dalek instead, with references made to a Dalek High Council. Frontier and Planet were set in the twenty-sixth century, while 'Death' refers to the recent 'Dalek Wars', and so presumably 'Death to the Daleks' follows on from the other two.

It might still have been plausible that all this was taking place prior to the events of 'The Daleks' and that the creatures seen there were remnants of a once-great empire. However, 'Planet of the Daleks' had Thals, who had become a space-faring race and also remembered legends of the Doctor's first encounter with the Daleks. Since the Daleks were an expansionist, interstellar power at this point, it marked a significant change to the end of the race shown in 1963 and explicitly contradicted the Doctor's reasoning in 'The Dalek Invasion of Earth'. For anyone following the series, this was all very confusing.

In 1975, Terry Nation revised the Daleks' origins in the serial 'Genesis of the Daleks', where the Doctor was sent by the Time Lords (or possibly their Celestial Intervention Agency) to the moment of the Daleks' creation, to stop the Dalek race before it could begin. In this story, the Dals were now called Kaleds (an anagram of Dalek), and the Dalek design attributed to one man, the crippled Kaled chief scientist and evil genius, Davros.

Instead of a short nuclear exchange, the Kaled-Thal war was

portrayed as a thousand-year-long war of attrition, fought with nuclear, biological and chemical weapons. When Davros deemed the mutations from the fallout irreversible, he experimented on living cells, treating them with chemicals and accelerating the mutations to discover the eventual Kaled mutation form and ensure its survival. These genetically conditioned forms were placed in tank-like travel machines, a design based on his own life-support chair. The Mark III travel machines, coupled with the mutants, became the first Daleks.

The Fourth Doctor's appearance on the scene (to try to prevent the creation of the Daleks, or at the very least, to lessen the damage they would do in future) led to the other Kaled scientists trying to shut down the Dalek project. To prevent this, Davros arranged for the Thals to wipe out his own people. The Daleks were then sent to exterminate the Thals, but later, they turned on Davros and apparently killed him. Sealing them in the Kaled bunker, the Doctor believed he had only retarded their progress by a thousand years.

Among fans, the most widespread theory, primarily because of its promulgation in *The Discontinuity Guide* by Paul Cornell, Martin Day and Keith Topping, is that the Doctor had succeeded in changing Dalek history. However, other commentators (such as Lawrence Miles in his reference work, *About Time*, and Lance Parkin in his chronology, *A History: An Unauthorised History of the Doctor of the Universe* and John Rocco Roberto's *The History of the Daleks*) argue that it is possible to reconcile the pre- and post-Genesis stories without the need to invoke two versions of Dalek history.

FROM CYBERMEN TO DALEKS

In any case, it is accurate to say that 'Genesis of the Daleks' marked a new era for the depiction of the species, with most of their previous history forgotten or barely referred to again. Future stories, which followed a rough story arc, also focused more on Davros, much to the dissatisfaction of some fans, who felt that the Daleks should take centre stage rather than becoming mere minions of their creator.

In 'Destiny of the Daleks' (1979), it was revealed that Davros had survived the Daleks' attack and lived on, buried in a bunker in suspended animation. While Davros was sleeping, the Daleks abandoned the ruins of Skaro and established a vast interstellar empire, eventually encountering a hostile race of androids called the Movellans. The Dalek and Movellan warfleets were very evenly matched and neither side's purely logical battle computers could find a successful strategy for an attack against the other. As a result, for centuries the two fleets remained locked in a stand-off, constantly manoeuvring and probing for an opportunity to break the stalemate, without either side firing a single shot.

The Daleks sent an expedition to the ruins of Skaro to recover Davros and seek his help in upgrading their designs in the hope of finding a way through the impasse, while the Movellans sent an expedition to stop them. But the Daleks succeeded in reviving Davros, who theorised the extreme intelligence and rationality of the battle computers were to blame and that the first side to take a seemingly reckless gamble would tip the balance in their favour. However, the Doctor intervened and prevented either the Dalek or Movellan expeditions from returning with this insight. Davros fell into the hands of a Human space empire and was put back in suspended animation for indefinite imprisonment.

This impasse continued for nearly a century until the Movellans finally developed a weapon capable of breaking it – a highly virulent biological agent that targeted Daleks. In 'Resurrection of the Daleks' (1984), having lost the war, the Daleks rescued Davros from the Human prison station, where he had been frozen for ninety years, and demanded that he should develop a defence against the disease. This time it was Davros who double-crossed the Daleks, deciding to take personal command of the Dalek race rather than merely serving it. His continuous influence eventually led to a schism among the Daleks, with one faction following Davros' leadership and another rejecting their creator to follow the Supreme Dalek instead.

By the time 'Revelation of the Daleks' came along in 1985, Davros was in hiding at the Tranquil Repose funeral facility on the planet Necros and carrying out experiments to physically transform humans into Daleks. He was also placing those Daleks loyal to him into white-and-gold casings to distinguish them from the usual black-and-grey Daleks, but his plans were undone when a worker at the facility contacted the original Daleks. They arrived on Necros, exterminated the white-and-gold Daleks and captured Davros, who was returned to Skaro to face trial.

Davros made his last televised appearance in the serial, 'Remembrance of the Daleks' in 1988. Apparently, events had taken place off-screen, as he appeared in the guise of the Dalek Emperor, leading his gold-and-white Imperial Daleks. At this point, Davros had modified the Imperial Daleks, adding cybernetic enhancements to their organic components. A new model – 'Special Weapons Dalek' – was introduced with an enormously powerful cannon and armour capable of deflecting regular Dalek weaponry. Also, for the first time, a Dalek was clearly seen onscreen to hover up a flight of stairs.

Pitted against the Imperial Daleks were the Renegade Daleks, led by a black Supreme Dalek. The name 'renegade' suggests the tables were turned and Davros' side had the upper hand. Both Dalek factions became aware that the Hand of Omega, a Gallifreyan stellar engineering device, was hidden on Earth in the year 1963. They sent expeditions to Earth, battling each other to retrieve it, hoping to use the Hand to create a power source that would refine their crude time travel technology.

Ultimately, the Imperial Daleks succeeded, not knowing that the Doctor had inserted a booby trap into the Hand's programming. When Davros activated it, Skaro's sun went supernova and both the Dalek homeworld and the Imperial Dalek fleet were destroyed. Davros, however, apparently escaped his flagship's destruction in an escape pod. The Renegade Dalek Supreme self-destructed when it was informed by the Doctor that it was the last-surviving Dalek.

'Remembrance of the Daleks' also marked the last on-screen appearance of the Daleks in the context of the programme until 2005, save for charity specials such as 'Doctor Who and the Curse of Fatal Death' and the use of Dalek voices in the *Doctor Who* television movie in 1996.

When *Doctor Who* was once again broadcast in 2005, many fans hoped the Daleks would return to the programme. After much negotiation between the BBC and the Nation estate (which at one point appeared to completely break down), an agreement was reached. Written by Rob Shearman, 'Dalek', the sixth episode of Series One, was shown on BBC1 on 30 April 2005. The new Dalek exhibited new features, including a swivelling mid-section that allowed it a 360-degree field of fire and a force field with the ability to disintegrate bullets before they struck it. As well as being able to fly, it could also regenerate itself by means of absorbing electrical power and the DNA of a Time Traveller. The 'plunger' manipulator arm could crush a man's skull, in addition to the technology interfacing abilities shown by earlier models. When the Dalek fired in a wet, metal room, its laser conducted like electricity. The Doctor described it as a 'genius', able to calculate a thousand billion lock combinations in a single second and to download the entire contents of the Internet. A more sophisticated model of the Dalek mutant also featured.

In 'Dalek', it was revealed that the Daleks and the Time Lords were involved in a Time War, in which the Doctor obliterated the entire Dalek race – all ten million ships of their fleet. The same war destroyed the Time Lords as well, with the Dalek appearing in the episode and the Doctor the only apparent survivors. Somehow the Dalek had fallen through time, ending up on Earth in the twenty-first century. By 2012, it had passed into the hands of American billionaire Henry van Statten, who dubbed it a 'Metaltron' and kept it in a secret underground museum called the Vault, along with other alien artifacts.

The Dalek was damaged, remaining silent and helpless, until the Ninth Doctor arrived at the Vault. Absorbing DNA from the Doctor's companion Rose Tyler, it regenerated itself and went on a killing spree. However, having done so, it continued to mutate and was beset with unfamiliar, human feelings. Realising it was now contaminated, the mutant asked Rose to order it to destroy itself, rather than continue to live in that way. It then disintegrated itself with an energy field created by the spheres along its lower casing.

The two-part 2005 series finale, comprising 'Bad Wolf' and 'The Parting of the Ways' revealed that this Dalek was, in fact, not the sole survivor of its race. The Emperor Dalek's ship also survived, falling through time in much the same way as the lone Dalek. Once hidden, it began to rebuild, infiltrating Earth society over the course of centuries and using human genetic material to create a new Dalek race. This Emperor (the script specifically stated it was not Davros) also came to see itself as a god and built its new society around the Daleks' worship of itself.

Subtly manipulating the Fourth Great and Bountiful Human Empire of the year 200,000 by means of news programmes transmitted from Satellite 5 in Earth orbit, the Daleks installed the monstrous Jagrafess as mankind's keeper. In 'The Long Game', the Doctor removed the Jagrafess, but was unaware the Daleks were behind it. Over the next one hundred years, the Daleks continued their scheme, recreating Satellite Five as the Game Station, acquiring more humans for mutation by subjecting them to twisted reality television games. The station's Controller was able to transport the Doctor and his companions into the station, where the Doctor discovered the presence of the Daleks. Now numbering close to half a million, the race was poised to invade Earth with a fleet of two hundred ships.

The Doctor built a Delta Wave projector that would wipe out the Daleks, but also eliminate all life on Earth and found himself unable to trigger it. However, Rose had absorbed energies from the spacetime vortex by staring into the heart of the Tardis and used those same energies to reduce the Daleks and their fleet to atoms.

In the 2006 series finale, 'Army of Ghosts' and 'Doomsday', it was revealed members of the Cult of Skaro (led by a black Dalek named Dalek Sec) had escaped during the Time War into the nothingness between dimensions – the Void – taking with them a Time Lord prison, dubbed the Genesis Ark, which contained millions of Daleks. The Daleks' Void Ship finally emerged in twenty-first century Earth to be examined by the Torchwood Institute. The path of the void ship also left a breach in space-time, which allowed the parallel Earth Cybermen to cross over into the Doctor's universe.

The Daleks rejected the Cybermen's proposal for an alliance to conquer the universe and the Ark was opened, releasing millions of Daleks to wage all-out war against the Cybermen across the planet. Ultimately, both armies were sucked back into the Void due to the actions of the Tenth Doctor. Sec, along with the other cult members, was able to initiate 'emergency temporal shift' before being sucked in.

David's favourite Dalek story is 'Genesis of the Daleks', the episode that introduced Davros, who interestingly enough, returned to the series for the first time in twenty years in the two final episodes of Series Four. It was the first time that David's incarnation of the Doctor had faced the megalomaniac scientist, who was last seen entering an escape pod in 1988. Now played by the Shakespearian actor Julian Bleach, the character planned to use his creations, the Daleks, to become the supreme ruler of the universe.

Horribly scarred and crippled after an explosion on his planet, Skaro, Davros had only one functioning arm and a robotic 'eye' mounted on his forehead. A master of robotics, the villain depended completely upon a self-designed mobile life-support chair, which enclosed the lower half of his body. As the story goes, this became the inspiration for his deadliest creation, the Daleks. But that wasn't the only surprise in store for the Series Four finale.

CHAPTER 10

NEW COMPANIONS

'Each script that we get is more funny and wilder and more inventive than the last. The show exists on several levels. It's an adventure story and it goes to some emotional places.'

(David taking about the *Doctor Who* scripts – 2007)

The first time viewers meet medical student Martha Jones is in the first episode of the third series broadcast on Saturday, 31 March 2007, when the hospital she works at is teleported to the Moon and alongside the Doctor, she helps save the day. In recognition of her help, he invites her to join him for a supposed single trip in his time machine, the Tardis, but later he accepts Martha as his full-time companion, admitting that she was never just a passenger, and he even gives her the key to the Tardis.

Nevertheless, Martha becomes frustrated because the Doctor remains oblivious to her feelings for him and she expresses concern that she is simply a rebound after the Doctor's painful loss of his previous companion, Rose. When the amnesiac Doctor falls in love in the 'Human Nature'/'The Family of Blood' two-parter, a pained Martha claims, 'You had to go and fall in love with a human … and it wasn't me.' In the series finale, in which the Doctor's nemesis, the Master, takes over planet Earth, capturing both the Doctor and fellow companion Captain Jack Harkness (played by John Barrowman), Martha is left alone to save the world. On the run from the Master, she spends a year travelling the world in a plan which restores the incapacitated Doctor and reverses time, undoing the Master's actions. Martha then leaves the Tardis of her own accord, telling the Doctor that she cannot waste her life pining after someone who doesn't feel the same way, but she promises that she will see him again.

Like Billie before her, Freema was full of praise for her co-star, David: 'He's a total joy, just as you might imagine him to be. He's full of energy and raring to go, and it's infectious. It's a real pleasure to be able to work with him and everyone on the show. That's work in inverted commas. I should call it game-playing, really.'

Filming for the third series began in August 2006, immediately after David finished filming the Christmas Special, 'The Runaway Bride' the previous month with a different companion, this time played by popular comedienne Catherine Tate, best known at that time for her character Lauren, the apathetic teenager who coined the catchphrase 'Am I bovvered?' Although viewers got their first glimpse of Tate in *Doctor Who* at the end of the 'Doomsday' episode after the Doctor lost Rose Tyler forever to another dimension, it would be almost six months before they would discover what she was doing aboard the Tardis at the end of Series Two.

Catherine played Donna Noble, who vanished just as she was about to get married, only to reappear in the Tardis console room – which of course, provided the storyline for the Christmas Special, in which the Doctor is faced with solving the riddle of how this virtually impossible feat was achieved, while simultaneously trying to return Donna to the church. Dashing through time and space to get her to the church on time, it becomes clear that she is the key to an ancient alien plan to destroy the earth. The episode ended with the Doctor inviting Donna to travel with him – an invitation she declined, or at least for the time being.

Interestingly enough, the idea for 'The Runaway Bride' had haunted Russell T. Davies since he was a child and he'd had the image of the Tardis whizzing past other vehicles on the motorway in pursuit of a particular car. It was not until 2004 that he learned that he might be able to bring it to life on the screen. During pre-production for Series Two, he discovered such a sequence could be achieved with special effects.

He suggested the chase scene could be included in Toby Whithouse's storyline for 'School Reunion', with the Doctor rescuing Sarah Jane Smith, but that would have derailed the script by taking too much time away from Sarah's development, so instead Davies opted to use it as the centrepiece for an episode of its own. He began work on a new storyline in which the Doctor and Rose are confronted by a mysterious bride, who appears in the Tardis.

Initially, 'The Runaway Bride' was intended to be the sixth episode of the 2006 season, following the 'Rise of the Cybermen' and 'The Age of Steel', but with the success of *Doctor*

Who's debut in March 2005, the idea quickly prompted a second season to be commissioned and also the programme's first-ever Christmas Special, 'The Christmas Invasion'. So phenomenally popular was the remainder of *Doctor Who*'s initial slate of adventures that at the BAFTA screening of 'The Parting Of The Ways' on 15 June 2005, it was announced that a third season and a second Christmas Special had already been given the green light. It was then that Davies decided to postpone 'The Runaway Bride' and instead to expand it to become the 2006 Christmas Special while episode three of Series Two, 'Tooth and Claw', was conceived to take its place.

In scripting the Special, Davies was faced with the challenge of how to handle the companion situation, given that Billie Piper was exiting *Doctor Who* in the second season finale 'Doomsday' and Freema Agyeman would replace her at the start of Series Three in March 2007. As he was not keen to introduce a new regular character into 'The Runaway Bride', preferring to defer this until the start of the 2007 season, he came across the solution much sooner than expected: he would make the eponymous bride a short-term companion, thereby bridging the gap between Rose and her successor, Martha Jones. One element that he initially intended to include in 'The Runaway Bride' was a climax set at the ancient stone monoliths of Stonehenge, but he was unable to come up with a satisfactory reasoning for Stonehenge's involvement and so the idea was subsequently abandoned.

Filming for 'The Runaway Bride' began on 4 July 2006. Unlike 'The Christmas Invasion', which was made as part of a larger production block alongside two adventures from the second season, it was agreed that this particular Special should form its own recording block that would, nonetheless, still mark the start of the new filming schedule that would also encompass the whole of the 2007 season.

According to Steve O'Brien's review in *SFX Magazine*, 'The Runaway Bride' picks up exactly where 'Doomsday' left off: after leaving Rose behind in a parallel universe, the Doctor returns to the Tardis to find Catharine Tate in his console room in her wedding dress, repeatedly screaming 'Where am I?' at the Doctor who cannot understand for the life of him, why she was beamed into the Tardis in the first place, especially, halfway through her wedding. It has to be an impossibility, but then again the Doctor has been around too long to believe that nothing is impossible. And so, in classic *Doctor Who* tradition, the race is on to get her to the church on time.

'In many ways,' wrote O'Brien, '*Doctor Who* had never really done anything like "The Runaway Bride" before. There's a bit of "The 39 Steps" in there and a heavy dumping of screwball comedy too. And at one point it suddenly becomes a Hollywood action movie ... Never in two years of peacock *Doctor Who* and in 26 years of pawn shop *Who* have we seen anything as jaw-slackening as this sequence. Russell T. Davies knows that for *Doctor Who* to compete on Christmas Day it has to run with its balls out to compete for people's attention in a pissed-up living room, in a way Saturday *Who* doesn't have to. When Sarah Parish's villain turns up it becomes as big and as visual as *Who's* ever been. It's a masterpiece of prosthetics and visual effects: slightly naff but at the same time brilliant.'

O'Brien also noted that although Catherine Tate is a curious celebrity – she wins awards and has hit TV shows – but there are still those that cannot warm to her, and others who positively dislike her. 'Her gnarly, sarky Donna won't win over those people, but it's she who really makes "The Runaway Bride" [even though] it doesn't have quite the festive feel of "The Christmas Invasion" – or feel so in love with the season.'

Like 'The Christmas Invasion', 'The Runaway Bride' was televised on Christmas Day as the highlight of the BBC's holiday line-up. Accruing only slightly fewer viewers than its predecessor, it once again rocketed *Doctor Who* into the week's Top 10 ratings. Although the show appeared to mark the end of Catherine Tate's involvement with *Doctor Who*, and despite what O'Brien noted, that many viewers could not warm to her, when Freema Agyeman unceremoniously left after finishing filming Series Three, Tate was asked if she would be interested in reprising her role as Donna to become the Doctor's new companion, his thirty-fifth sidekick, for Series Four; a part that she was more than happy to accept.

In fact, earlier, at the press screening of 'The Runaway Bride', when Catherine was asked whether or not she would like to become the Doctor's companion, she replied, 'I would love to, but no one has asked'. And when they did ask, a little over six months later, she was literally over the moon: 'I am delighted to be returning to *Doctor Who*. I had a blast last Christmas and look forward to travelling again through time and space with that nice man from Gallifrey.'

Russell T. Davies was equally delighted to have her back on board: 'Catherine was an absolute star in "The Runaway Bride" and we are delighted that one of Britain's greatest talents has agreed to join us for the fourth series.' Yet there were still critical objections to the decision to bring her back for an entire series. As Daniel Martin noted in his 'TV and radio blog' for the *Guardian,* if he had been asked to write about the fact that Catherine Tate would be returning to *Doctor Who*, as the Doctor's new companion for Series Four, he would, he said, have raged the same kind of fury that was appearing elsewhere on the Internet. 'I would have written words I would now have to eat: that this would be the moment where the show would jump the shark; that this disaster would be Catherine Tate's fault.'

Of course the decision to recruit Tate again may have caused some frothing at the mouth among fans, but whereas some were less than pleased that Donna Noble from 'The Runaway Bride' would be returning, and according to Martin, would be a 'braying annoyance and that she would ruin the series with her wailing', others believed perhaps it wasn't all bad news. As Martin later reflected, if the general consensus was that 'The Runaway Bride' was by far the weakest Christmas Special, and even if Davies himself had once commented that a character like Donna would annoy viewers across an entire season, there were those who still swore 'they would never watch again. But everyone, it seemed, missed the point. By the end of "The Runaway Bride", Donna had, in today's TV parlance, gone on a journey. She wasn't the screeching irritant we encountered at the start of the episode. And to be fair, if you were inexplicably teleported into a spaceship while walking down the isle, you'd screech as well.'

It seemed a lot of the objection stemmed from the fact that Tate was so obviously not 'for the dads' as, say, Billie Piper or Freema Agyeman had been, but did that matter? Davies was probably the key member of the *Doctor Who* team who thought not, and he in turn reacted angrily to the criticism. He told *SFX Magazine*: 'The doubts about her, as far as I can see, are fundamentally stupid. They say she's going to shout her way through the whole thing. They say she shouted her way through "The Runaway Bride". No, she didn't. Literally, factually, no matter of opinion, no, she did not.'

Ultimately, it seemed as if Donna's character would put a nice new spin on things: 'For once, she's not in love with the Doctor – the ruin of the brilliant Martha Jones,' and although the relationship was likened to that of Spencer Tracy and Katharine Hepburn's on-screen romances, it would probably be more correct to say that most regarded Donna more as a big sister than a love interest, which according to Martin, has to be welcomed. In turn, David himself offered the view that a no-nonsense Donna would, after all, 'keep his feet on the ground a bit. The Doctor had a slight tendency to be little pompous, but she cuts through that.'

Once again, the fourth series offered up the usual amount of surprises and twists and turns as the previous seasons. According to one reviewer, Scott Matthewman of *The Stage*, the fourth episode, 'The Unicorn and the Wasp', written by Gareth Roberts, was the best edition of the show since it started in 1963 and unlike any other *Doctor Who* story in the history of the programme. It was, the reviewer claimed, 'a glorious combination of melodrama, comedy and high tension,' which received an overnight audience rating of 7.7 million, making it the most successful episode of the series since 'The Fires of Pompeii', the second episode of the new series that was shown five weeks earlier.

Indeed, from the moment the guests start arriving at Lady Eddison's Eddison Hall country manor, wrote Matthewman, trouble is already afoot. 'In true Agatha Christie style, all the characters refer to each other by their full names in ways that nobody ever does in real life. And when the delightfully named Professor Peach slopes off to the library, we know that he's unlikely to survive to see the opening titles. That he is offed by a giant wasp brandishing a piece of lead piping is gloriously ridiculous, blending a comedic *Cluedo* reference with *Doctor Who's* more traditional alien menace in a seamless manner that sums up the episode as a whole.'

However, Mark Wright, another reviewer for *The Stage*, wasn't so impressed with the start of the episode one week earlier. 'With a title as contentious as *The Doctor's Daughter*, one can't help but feel cheated within the first three minutes of this episode when the cute pouty girl we've seen trailed endlessly during the week isn't actually the Doctor's daughter, but a knock off bit of DNA created at the top of the episode.'

All the same, he confessed, the next 45 minutes turned out to be much better than he expected when the Tardis is drawn to the planet Messaline, depositing the Doctor, Donna and Martha in the midst of a war between human colonists and the piscene Hath which has been waging for generations. Martha is kidnapped by the Hath, while the Doctor and Donna discover that the humans breed by accelerated progenation: recombining a single individual's DNA to produce a new, adult person, ready for battle. Subjected to this process, the Doctor abruptly comes face to face with his daughter, Jenny, as Donna begins to discover that there is more to the war on Messaline than meets the eye.

At the end of the episode the Doctor takes Martha home. Martha warns Donna that life with the Doctor can be dangerous, but Donna nevertheless resolves to stay with the Doctor indefinitely. Concurrently, on Messaline, Jenny revives in front of a Hath. She escapes Messaline, resolving to follow in her father's footsteps by resolving disputes and fighting villains. As Wright said in his review, 'one can't help but feel that we haven't seen the last of Jenny, the Doctor's daughter'.

Nor, it seemed had David – well, not off-screen, at any rate. Soon after the episode aired it was revealed he was dating Georgia Moffett, who played his on-screen daughter. She had originally auditioned for the part of Rose Tyler for the first series in 2005, and had lost out to Billie Piper; she tried again for a role in 'The Unicorn and the Wasp' episode, but was again unsuccessful. However, like Freema Agyman before her, she impressed the producers so much that, as a result, she was offered a more substantial role – that of the Doctor's daughter.

She remembers, 'It was winter in Cardiff when we filmed and I was wearing very little, so you can imagine how cold that was. David kindly lent me his jacket between takes. I put it on, bent over and ripped the back of it. He's a good 6 foot-something and he's never ripped it; I'm 5 foot 2, put it on and destroyed it! I spent the whole five weeks I was doing it in a daze that I was there. I didn't quite believe it. I still don't quite believe it. The first day I arrived there they took me to Make-Up via the inside of the Tardis. I was just going, "oh my God!".'

In many ways, her romance with David promised to be one of those showbiz relationships made in tabloid heaven that come along every once in a while and get every journalist in the land excited at the prospect. It had started when David and Georgia were photographed leaving Cardiff's premier five-star St David's Hotel and Spa, and later from David's North London house after spending the night together and then again, from Georgia's West London home in Twickenham (where she has lived since 2006), after an overnight stay.

It was tabloid news, firstly because of the age gap between David and Georgia, and secondly because she was, interestingly enough, the real-life daughter of Peter Davison, who had played the Time Lord from 1982 to 1984. Matters weren't helped by the fact that she was David's fourth known conquest from the programme's cast and crew since he had landed the role three years earlier.

According to an insider from the set of *Doctor Who*, it seemed this could be just the tip of the iceberg: 'There have been at least five and probably more – but he's just so darned charming everybody still loves him to bits.' Richard Price, writing in the

Daily Mail, spoke to an undisclosed source: 'David may not have the looks of Brad Pitt, [but] he is an absolute genius when it comes to impressing women, and he's having the time of his life. He spends a lot of time filming the show in Wales and let's just say there has been a lot of traffic through his apartment in Cardiff Bay. He takes women to St David's Hotel because it's quiet, luxurious and the staff love him there.' Not only that, but the hotel's employees are renowned for their polite attentiveness. And when it comes to a valued customer like David, they are aware that it really doesn't do to pry.

All the same, continued the *Doctor Who* source, 'it has become a standing joke that you never know who David will walk through the door with next. Some of the staff has been having bets on whether it will be a blonde or a brunette. But the most extraordinary thing is he manages to stay on good terms with everyone. Maybe it's his Scottish charm or the fact he is a decent man, but somehow he manages to square the circle and keep everyone happy.'

As one admiring member of the crew put it, 'Where does he find the time, let alone the energy? To see David in action with people in general, and with women in particular, is a work of art in motion. He is such a charmer that he can get away with anything; he always has time for everyone and the women love that. If there are any children who come to filming, David always makes a fuss of them and poses for family pictures. The women love him on the set – he could have his pick of most of the single girls – and probably a few of the married ones, too, if he wanted.

'It's a bit sickening for the blokes, though. You would love to hate anyone that good with women – but even the men have to like him as well. There's a few gay guys around and they love him just as much, but they reluctantly accept he's a devout heterosexual – and practising very hard at it from what I can see. He's been in the gossip columns about going out with a few girls on the set, but believe me, that is not the whole story. I know he's been out with at least another two girls. It may have just been for a late-night coffee – they're too discreet to kiss and tell – but they were very happy about it.'

But another member of the *Doctor Who* team insists David's roving eye is down to the high intensity on set, where working days regularly run from dawn until dusk. Friends who have known him for longer, though, suggest there may be another, altogether more deep-rooted explanation – his upbringing: 'David may be regarded as something of a lothario these days, but there is nothing he would like more than to fall madly in love and settle down to a lifetime of monogamy,' says a friend, who has known him since his early days at the Royal Scottish Academy of Music and Drama.

'The problem is that his romantic ideal is so hard to attain. His parents were an amazingly dedicated couple and he idolised them. So far he hasn't met the right girl – but in this day and age the notion of being married for the best part of half a century is a bit unrealistic. He needs to learn to compromise, perhaps ease off on the work so he can get his personal life in order, but that's not David. His expectations in life are ridiculously high, which is probably why he's so successful.'

Intriguingly for someone so ostentatiously successful with the opposite sex, during the early years of his career tongues wagged about David's sexuality – partly fuelled by his relaxed attitude to the rumours. When he was at drama school, several of his contemporaries believed erroneously that he was gay. Much the same as when he lived with Arabella Weir. 'In the early days many of my friends (principally male, I'll admit), thought that he must be gay. "He has to be – you're his best friend, and look at the way he dresses," they'd protest. Leaving aside the suggestion that an association with me reflects on a man's sexuality, I had to break it to them that just because a guy wears a red velvet suit and is able to form a close friendship with a woman he isn't sleeping with doesn't necessarily mean he's homosexual. David, meanwhile, took all this teasing in his stride; he is so unmacho and fair-minded that the speculation about his sexuality never bothered him. "Why would it?" he'd say.'

David simply ignored the gay rumours, much the same as he ignored any tittle-tattle about his love life that was doing the rounds. As journalist Richard Price noted in his *Daily Mail* piece, friends say he is unconcerned about them. One suggested they were a handy way of dampening down speculation about the amount of time he spends with attractive young women. One female member of the *Doctor Who* crew, who asked Price not to be named, said gossip about his sexuality was hilarious. 'It's hard to put into words how charming he is,' gushed the twenty-something blonde. 'David has huge brown eyes and when he turns the full glare on you then no girl with a pulse is going to get away from him. He may look stringy and geeky, but that man has more sex appeal than anyone I've ever met. He's the nicest man in showbusiness.'

This is not an isolated opinion, continued Price: 'Tales of the *DoctorWho* star's largesse abound and he has a deserved reputation as a star who has not lost the common touch. On one occasion, when recording a voiceover for a documentary, he was approached while having lunch by a minion who worked with disadvantaged children in his spare time. When the man explained that his charges were big fans of *DoctorWho*, David spent the entire break recording an improvised skit in character as the Time Lord on a mobile phone camera.

'Friends say it is this spontaneous generosity of spirit [he neither sought nor received publicity for the gesture], coupled with unshakeable self-belief, which makes him so irresistible to women. In Georgia Moffett, however, some suggest he may have taken on more than he bargained for. Unlike David, her parents – actors Sandra Dickinson and Peter Davison – had complicated relationships.'

Dickinson and Davison were married to other people when they met, and by the time their marriage dissolved after 14 years, it had descended into a series of bitter rows. Today they are barely on speaking terms and friends say this, coupled with the startling fact that at twenty-three, Georgia already has a six-year-old son, has left its mark on her. How long the romance with David will endure remains to be seen. Since being photographed together, they have both have been keeping a relatively low profile. A mutual friend agrees: 'It's early days for David and Georgia and

I'm not sure if it will go anywhere. He's almost 15 years older than her and besides their profession, they don't have a huge amount in common.'

Even some of David's admirers will admit that he has a steely side. One TV interviewer who has known him for years says that since landing the *Doctor Who* role, he has developed the celebrity tic of referring to himself in the third person: 'There is an egotism and ruthlessness about him. The most important person in David Tennant's life is himself, which means he isn't ideal boyfriend material. So long as it's convenient he'll make a woman feel as if she's the only girl in the world. But career comes first.' But as his former landlady Arabella Weir attests, 'Steeliness is his defining characteristic,' and many believe it is this unwavering commitment to his career that has rendered him incapable of sustaining long-term relationships.

As the article concluded, those who have known him for longer, however, point to the impossibly high standards set by his parents' wonderful 45-year union. 'He still firmly believes that one day he'll meet someone special and they'll be together for ever,' says an old college friend. 'But that's not going to happen if he changes girlfriends as often as his socks.'

Although, as more or less expected, the reviews for the fourth series of *Doctor Who* found very little fault with any episode, it is hard not to speculate on what the reaction would be to a future one-off special, if the rumours were to be believed. Although the Doctor was barely in the 'Turn Left' episode that was shown in the lead up to the finale of Series Four, this would be the first episode in the series' history not to feature the Doctor at all. Instead, the Time Lord's three female assistants, Rose, Martha and Donna, would take the starring roles. The shock twist comes after the Doctor gets lost in space and his faithful sidekicks, played by Billie Piper, Freema Agyeman and Catherine Tate, are left to take control of the Tardis as they battle to save the world from an alien invasion, which in part sounded as if it could have been the template for the 'Journey's End' finale. According to an insider at the show's top-secret Cardiff set, 'The chemistry between the three assistants is electric. It is so strong that we realised the Doctor could be in danger of getting in the way so it is left to the girls to sort things out, having to save civilisation and the Doctor himself.'

All the same, the insider added, 'It is a bit of a gamble having *Doctor Who* without the Doctor, it has never been done before. But everyone is so interested in the different assistants that it should be fantastic. Donna, Martha and Rose are all competing for his attention in different ways and all want to be the best.'

According to the spoilers that appeared on the Internet two weeks before the series ended, it sounded very much like the finale, in which 'the girls' and a small army of the Time Lord's other companions, past and present, do in fact, have to save the Doctor, the Tardis and the rest of the universe from Davros's new empire of Daleks.

But it was the penultimate episode, 'The Stolen Earth', that caused the biggest stir among fans and the general viewing public, when, in the final scenes, the Doctor was wounded by a Dalek and started the regeneration process, which, in turn, got the whole country wondering who would replace him – how and when. But as the producer of the behind-the-scenes *Doctor Who Confidential* explained after 'Journey's End' had been seen by an estimated 9.4 million viewers, grabbing 45 percent of the total television audience, 'he regenerates, but he channels the energy into his hand so he comes back as himself'.

Even so, it was a huge gamble to bring him back from his mid-regeneration unchanged, as it had never been done before in the history of the show and could have quite easily started an outrage among fans, who may have also insisted that such a regeneration was not possible. But then, as one journalist noted, when you have such an immense cliffhanger from the previous week, the usual rules just fly out the window.

The BBC went to great lengths to keep the twists and turns of the final episode under wraps for an entire week, in which, among other things, the Doctor was cloned allowing his assistant Donna, played by Catherine Tate, to absorb some of his mind to become a half Time Lord and save the day from the Daleks almost single-handedly. In the end, though, the Doctor leaves his half-human cloned-self with Billie Piper in the parallel universe she had returned from. It was predicted that one of his companions would die, but in the end none did. But that didn't stop the script demanding that Tate should end up being separated from her hero and having her mind wiped of all her memories so that the Doctor could depart in the Tardis, this time on his own, to re-emerge six months later for the 2008 Christmas Special with David Morrisey, Dervla Kirwan and newcomer Velile Tshabalala.

Above: Filming in Cardiff Bay with Freema Agyeman, the actress who was first seen playing David's companion, Martha Jones, in Series 3 of *Doctor Who* in March 2007.

© *REX Features*

Below left: With a Dalek at a special promotional screening of *Doctor Who*. © *REX Features*

Below right: Playing Buttons in the Virgin Radio Christmas Pantomime, December 2006.

© *PA Photos*

Cleaning up at the BAFTA Cymru Awards. *Doctor Who* and its spin-off *Torchwood* picked up twelve awards between them at the 2007 ceremony. David is shown here with *Torchwood*'s Eve Myles.

David Tennant was the second guest host in the sixth series of *The Friday Night Project*. He is seen here, alongside Alan Carr and Justin Lee Collins, in a sketch imagining that he is his father many years ago (*above*), as a new camp Doctor in a spoof of *Doctor Who* (*below left*), and as Celeb BB5 contestant 'H' (*below right*).

© *PA Photos*

Above: Introducing the Pussycat Dolls at the Live Earth concert in London, July 2007.

© *Getty Image*

With Sophia Myles, at the premiere of *Harry Potter and the Order of the Phoenix* (*below left*), and snuggling up in the stands at Wembley Arena to watch the Live Earth concert (*below right*).

© *REX Feature*

bove: On stage at the Dominion Theatre making a guest appearance in *The Fast Show ive*, November 2007.

© *Getty Images*

elow left: Filming *Doctor Who* in Cardiff Bay.

© *REX Features*

elow right: Making an appearance at the Science Museum in London for a gala screening 'Voyage of the Damned', the 2007 Christmas Special of *Doctor Who*.

© *PA Photos*

Above: Signing autographs outside the *Radio Times Party*, London, January 2008.

Below: With Lenny Henry, John Simms, Kate McGowan, and other friends, at Jools Holland's 2007 Hootenanny.

© *REX Features*

resenting friend and 'Voyage of the Damned' co-star, Kylie Minogue, with the Brit
ward for Best International Female, at the Brits in London, February 2008.

Above: Plugging the latest series of *Doctor Who* on the Capital Radio Breakfast Show

Below: Fooling around on *Friday Night with Jonathan Ross* alongside his *Doctor Who* Series 4 co-star, Catherine Tate.

Whereas most viewers had, in the past, been content to wait a week for each new episode, the penultimate episode was so filled with excitement that there were reports of literally millions of fans surfing the Internet to try and find out what might be coming, and who the next Doctor would be. But there was no information to be found on the web, in the press, or elsewhere; it remained one of the best kept secrets in British television. It helped that absolutely no preview copies of the show were sent out. Not to journalists or to any of the hundreds of people who worked on the programme.

One of David's former assistants, Freema Agyeman, believes the final episode of Series Four was 'the secret of all secrets.' She was amazed at the response after 7.4 million people tuned in to watch 'The Stolen Earth'. She said she received tonnes of text messages and everywhere she went people were coming up to her in the street asking if David was leaving.

Although Freema appeared in three of the episodes, giving the Doctor two companions midway through the fourth series, and then came back for the big two finale episodes, according to the actress, Martha and the Doctor have still got a friendship, 'but there's somebody else in Martha's life now so she doesn't need the Doctor in that respect. That part of her soul has been fulfilled; that attraction has dissipated and it's quite professional. It's nice to see how they've moved on, because she did feel quite strongly about him. Altogether, she decided not to travel with him any more because of how she felt and it wasn't returned, so it's great to see her move on from that to value his friendship enough to still want him around. It's one of the reasons why *Doctor Who* is so popular, because of the emotional believability of the characters, and that's why Martha had to leave at the end [of Series Three]. She went through a year of travelling the world alone through hardship, while her family were imprisoned and tortured, so it really hardened her up. It's not something she can forget and revert back to her old self.'

In fact, when viewers meet Martha again for the first time in Series Four, 'we don't know how much time has passed since she left the Tardis,' explains Freema. 'She is still interested in alien incursions and is now working for UNIT. She's qualified and has this important position there.'

Billie Piper's appearance at the end of the first episode of Series Four, 'Partners in Crime', was not quite so significant. She simply appeared for a few seconds, only to vanish again, as if to suggest something larger was going on. As well as setting up the mystery, this also ties the end of the episode up with its start – the idea that the Doctor is always around the corner from something, or someone, of interest. Of course, many reviewers asked the same question: why did Rose vanish and why was she there in the first place?

Interestingly enough, Billie admitted that she was nervous about reprising her role, especially for the last three episodes, because she said she had forgotten how to play the character! 'I am a bit worried about getting back into the groove. I was shocked and saddened the other day when I tried playing Rose Tyler to myself, in my bathroom, and I couldn't do it. I tried and tried, and it had gone [but] hopefully not for good.'

She was also feeling slightly disappointed to miss out on a chance to work with Kylie on the 2007 Christmas Special: 'I want to reclaim David Tennant as my own, after he's been working with Kylie,' she laughed. 'I'm gutted I missed her. I speak to David and he brags about how he has her number in his phone. I want to be Kylie's friend!' Who wouldn't want to be best pals with someone who is just so simply delightful in every way? But Billie didn't feel quite the same affection towards Freema when she took over as the Doctor's companion in Series Three. Well, she didn't to start with, at any rate. Now, she recalls, 'I thought I would feel really jealous towards her, but it's been fine. I had been replaced. Life goes on.'

Despite David's friendship with Kylie, and even after he presented the diminutive star with her gong for 'Best International Female Artist' at the 2008 Brits, Billie and David were still thoroughly enamored with each other, and remained the best of friends. 'I see him quite a lot, we are really good mates,' she was quick to reply, when asked. 'I like everything about him, which makes it really easy to be in his company. He's a sweet, sweet guy. I call him to ask him all my acting questions and he always supports what I do.'

He would even attend Billie's wedding on 31 December 2007 to fellow actor Laurence Fox when the pair tied the knot in a 50-minute ceremony at the Parish Church of St Mary's in Easebourne, West Sussex. According to the tabloid press, Billie, then just twenty-five, wore a low-cut ivory formal wedding dress with a black coat draped over her shoulders and was accompanied by four bridesmaids in short purple dresses.

Billie, who was five minutes early for the wedding, which took place about half a mile from the couple's £750,000 home in Midhurst, was welcomed by the bridegroom, who had arrived 45 minutes before the ceremony was due to start. Flanked by friends, he made the short walk from the White Horse pub to the church, past the throng of photographers and reporters.

Dressed in a flamboyant burgundy velvet suit, David, who turned up without a guest, even though he was said to have been dating Bethan Britton at the time, arrived at the church – around the same time as Kevin Whately – to cheers from the public, who had already lined the road leading to the church.

Laurence and Billie had met each other in December 2006 when together they performed in a stage production of Christopher Hampton's *Treats* that ended after six weeks of doing the provincial rounds at the Garrick Theatre in London in February 2007. Interestingly enough, it was David who had convinced her to try some theatre in the first place. Today she says it was an amazing experience and it was all down to David for making her do it. But then again, David 'absolutely loves [the stage]', enthuses Billie.

'He kept telling me these stories and it just sounded so good, like being back in drama school again. I've been leaning on him a lot,' she said. She asked him all sorts of questions about how she was going to deal with her opening press night at the Garrick. 'He said, "You can't really talk someone down from the ledge if they're there. It's just something they've got to go through." And he's right. He's a serious thesp. He must've done at least a dozen massive press nights, so he should know what he's talking about.'

In many ways, through his encouragement David was responsible for Billie doing the play. So, in a round about sort of way, you could say he could take credit for her getting together with Laurence. If she had not taken his advice, she may never have met him and ended up as happily married as she is said to be. Just one year after the nerve-wracking press night that Billie sought David's advice for, in April 2008, the *Sun,* quoting an unnamed source, announced that Billie was three months pregnant. By all accounts she and Laurence were absolutely over the moon.

CHAPTER 11

UNDER PRESSURE

'She made me first realise the possibilities of great literature
– J.D. Salinger, Harper Lee, Orwell and Arthur Miller. And
guided me towards a dim understanding of what Shakespeare
could be about.'

(David talking about his English teacher – 2005)

Two months before the biggest *Doctor Who* episode yet, the
Christmas Day Special with Kylie Minogue, was shown on
BBC1, David called time on his relationship with Sophia Myles. He
was said to have ended the romance by phone while his girlfriend
was working in Los Angeles and he was filming in Britain.
According to the *News of the World,* one of the reasons for the break-
up was the distance between them now that she had moved to live
on the West Coast of America; the one thing that he didn't want, it
transpired, was a long distance relationship. The phone call had
apparently left Sophia devastated. For her, it was a complete shock
and she just hadn't seen it coming. 'He just called and said it was all

over,' she apparently told friends. 'He stressed that there was no one else and it was just one of those things.'

One year earlier, Sophia had told friends how happy she was to be with David and how she wanted to start a family with him. But David, of course, at the time of their break-up, had been nursing his own wounds after he lost his mother to cancer. As a 'friend' revealed, 'It's a difficult time for David, maybe he just needs some space. It's a shame because they made a lovely couple.' The pair first met, albeit briefly, in 2002, on the set of the ITV crime drama *Foyle's War,* during the making of the third episode, 'A Lesson in Murder', even though they did not have any scenes together. They didn't hook up again until three years later, when Sophia filmed the *Doctor Who* episode, 'The Girl in the Fireplace' in which she played the role of Madame de Pompadour. Reportedly, that is when she fell for David, both during and after filming.

But now, after three years of being together, David's life with Sophia had ended, and although he was the one to kill it off, it is still interesting to look back over Sophia's career at the time of their breaking up. By then it had almost been 10 years since she began her route to screen stardom. She was spotted in a school play and cast in a BBC version of *The Prince and the Pauper* in 1996. Since then, she had roles in the 1999 television adaptation of *Oliver Twist* and appeared in films such as *The Abduction Club* (2002), with Alice Evans, and *From Hell* (2001), in which she played Johnny Depp's wife. Although by that time a rising star, Sophia remained delightfully modest, and still does to this day: 'I've never had a career plan. I came into this business by fluke when I was spotted in the school play,' she says. 'I never get recognised. Maybe it's because I look so different from job to job, so I can go round the supermarket without a care in the world; I could go round with a T-shirt that said my name and no one would notice.'

Five years earlier, it was a different story, however, when she found herself unemployed and desperate – until a brush with vampirism brought her career back from the dead. By then, the TV roles and film bit-parts had pretty much dried up, and she had been on the dole for 18 months, 8 of them spent learning how to ice-skate for a Michelle Pfeiffer film, which later collapsed due to a lack of finance for the production. 'Even though I was skint, I managed to get a credit card and I bought the cheapest one-way ticket to LA I could find,' she recalls. Her first audition was for *Underworld* (2003): 'I got that job, which was my salvation. I played a vampire called Erika, who was a feisty little minx.' Little did she know then that history would repeat itself when, three years later, she landed the role of a sex-hungry vampire in the BBC's terrifying adaptation of Bram Stoker's *Dracula*.

Similarly to Francis Ford Coppola's 1992 film version that promised to be the real story of the vampire king, with the cream of young Hollywood at the time, including Gary Oldman, Winona Ryder and Keanu Reeves, the BBC production also seemed destined to blow the cobwebs off traditional period drama with its predominantly youthful cast headed by Marc Warren as a surprisingly Byronic Count Dracula and Rafe Spall as Jonathan Harker.

'It was very lavish and sexy in a way I don't think the BBC has seen before,' Sophia said excitedly. She played Lucy, the nubile bride of Lord Holmwood, who has syphilis and can't consummate their relationship without infecting his wife. 'Lucy is twenty-one and ripe for the picking; she's sexually confident and hungry for sexual exploration.' She admits, 'I didn't have any confidence when I was her age, whereas Lucy loves the fact that she has blossomed into a woman. So when her husband won't sleep with her, she develops a wandering eye.' Holmwood summons a Transylvanian aristocrat, who has the ability to cure ills with transfusions of his blood, but when Dracula arrives, he seduces Lucy to the ranks of the undead.

Indeed, by the time Sophia was twenty-six, her love life had become almost as well known as her acting: in 2004 she was involved in an over-publicised affair with Charles Dance; in 2005, before her and David became romantically involved, she was linked to Damian Lewis. When her and David took things a step further, after meeting again on the *Doctor Who* set, she was ready to tell everyone how happy she was about it, even disclosing the fact that she was thrilled to be carrying one of the new Doctor dolls in her bag: 'I'm pretty excited that my boyfriend has an action doll. How cool!' she said at the time. 'Yes, I am stupidly in love, and it's all brilliant.'

But, like David, she was careful not to give away too much about her relationship. Her close friends Orlando Bloom, Keira Knightley and Sienna Miller had all cautioned her about revealing too much. 'Once you take your relationship into the public arena, it's a bit like dancing with the Devil, and you should expect to suffer the consequences,' she said.

David agreed: 'The trouble is, if you start talking about this stuff

– I know because I have in the past – by the time the article comes out, if the information has changed, you end up looking like such an arse, so it's my policy not to. You've got to be very careful because as soon as you enter the arena of all that stuff you've got to know what you're giving up. As soon as you start talking about certain things you make yourself fair game, don't you?'

Soon after David broke up with Sophia, she returned from Hollywood to live in Green Park, London, to continue her career in films and television, for which she has won several awards, including a Best Actress Scottish BAFTA for her role in *Hallam Foe,* which started a limited release in US theatres in June 2008. By all accounts, she didn't remain alone for long. Since splitting with David, she is said to have dated Holly Valance's one-time beau, Australian actor Alex O'Loughlin, and Paul Wilson, the bass guitarist of Snow Patrol, an Irish band which, ironically enough, were formed in Scotland.

It was one month after breaking up with Sophia that David was back on the small screen in a special five-minute *Doctor Who* mini-episode sketch for the 2007 Children In Need appeal. 'Time Crash', written by Steven Moffat and directed by Graeme Harper, teamed him up with Peter Davison, who had played the fifth Doctor for two years from 1982.

As executive producer Julie Gardner told the *Doctor Who Magazine*, '*Doctor Who* has a history of wonderful association with Children In Need, and everyone was keen for that to continue in 2007. Every year, we've tried to do something different. In 2005, we had the Charity Dinner and the first scene between the Tenth

Doctor and Rose, last year saw the concert of Murray Gold's music at the Wales Millennium Centre, so we decided that the only way to top that was with two Doctors! The planning and a lot of people gave their time up on a Sunday to shoot the scene. We hope that the *Doctor Who* viewers will have fun, and support Children In Need in every way possible.'

In fact, one of the great things about the mini-episode was how it seamlessly fitted into the gap between the Series Three finale, 'Last of the Time Lords', and the then upcoming Christmas Special, 'Voyage of the Damned'.

It ran for about seven minutes and picked up from when Martha leaves the Tardis at the end of Series Three. The mini-episode moves inside the Tardis, where it seems the Doctor is still encountering a problem. That is when the Fifth Doctor appears in the console room. The Tenth Doctor is gleeful at the meeting, but the Fifth Doctor is initially baffled, assuming his future incarnation is a deranged fan. But, as the Tenth Doctor explains, he forgot to put the shields up after rebuilding the Tardis and as a consequence it has collided with the Fifth Doctor's Tardis in a time stream.

This, the Tenth Doctor says, is generating a paradox at the heart of the ship, which is powerful enough to rip a hole in the universe the exact size of Belgium. Without a further thought, the Tenth Doctor fiddles the Tardis controls to manipulate a supernova into exact counterbalance; it cancels out the black hole caused by the paradox, so that all matter remains constant. This amazes the Fifth Doctor, before he quickly realises that the Tenth Doctor came up with the solution only because he remembered this encounter from an earlier episode. The Fifth Doctor says his farewells, and the Tenth Doctor tells the Fifth of the personality traits that he retained from his Fifth self (trainers, the altering pitch of his voice, and his spectacles), and also tells him how he loved being him and that he was 'his Doctor'. As he departs, the Fifth Doctor reminds the Tenth to raise his shields again, but it appears that he was too late, the hull of the *Titanic* has already crashed through one of the walls of the Tardis, as was originally seen at the end of Series Three.

As Phil Collinson explained to Benjamin Cook when he caught up with the producer for a *Doctor Who Magazine* feature in December 2007, the idea for 'Time Crash' had been something they had wanted to do for some time. 'I can't remember when we decided to do a Fifth and Tenth Doctor mini-episode, but I don't think we ever talked about doing anything else, really. Peter was my Doctor. I remember that time so clearly. When he took over, the show had a new lease of life. It felt like a show that would never end. Peter was brilliant, and I loved all the companions that he had. After Sarah Jane, Tegan is probably my favourite companion ever. Obviously, you wonder if it's going to work now, and Peter is a few years older, but he looks just like the Doctor that I remember, and he jumped straight back into playing it. We all have such fondness for those old days of the series. There's never any sense that we're ashamed of it, or we try to hide from it. We're genuinely in awe of and grateful to those people, so Peter coming back for this Children in Need scene is thrilling.'

It also seemed that David was in awe of Davison. Certainly, revealed Davison, he was nervous around him when filming the mini-episode one Sunday afternoon in early October 2007. 'David and I very much got on and did the scene. I only found out afterwards that he was a fan of my Doctor, because he sent me a very nice text saying that he was at first a bit tongue-tied. I wasn't aware of that at all!' But it was, he added enormous fun to make even though he felt his cricket-inspired costume was initially a little out of place in the new Tardis set, but he apparently grew into it again after and hour or so.

It was soon after *Children In Need* aired on 16 November 2007 that David was once again seen on BBC1, this time in a one-off comedy drama filmed the previous April during a break from *Doctor Who*. Scripted by co-star, Jessica Hynes, *Learners* followed the trials and tribulations of a group of learner drivers, with David playing a driving instructor called Chris, who finds himself the hot apex of a love triangle. 'He's a very decent chap, though,' said David. 'But he is perhaps not the most glamorous man alive, but he's very dependable. His confidence as a driving instructor is not matched by his confidence as a human being, really. But he's a passionate driving instructor, he's very good at it, and it's vocational for him.'

Bev (played by Hynes) is a downtrodden wife, who has failed her driving test eight times. She's desperate to pass yet frustrated by her husband Ian's impatient approach when teaching her to drive. When she meets glamorous driving-school owner Fiona, played by Sarah Hadland, she is determined to succeed, along with a group of other learner drivers.

Chris, a devout Christian with the patience of a saint, is assigned her instructor and it's not long before Bev develops a crush on him. He, however, harbours feelings for Fiona, but she's having an affair with a married man named Gerry, who works with Bev. It turned out that Haynes had more than just a passing interest in scripting the story: 'It took me 10 years to pass my test, and this year I finally did it so I could do the film! I had a great instructor, he taught me to take my time and relax. When I passed I cried with joy!'

As far as David was concerned, one of the good things about *Learners* was that he could fit it in around his *Doctor Who* filming schedule as he was only required to film his scenes for a couple of weeks. Interestingly enough, by the time *Learners* aired in November 2007, he had more or less completed 2 series of 13 episodes each of *Doctor Who* plus two Christmas Specials.

Compared to *Doctor Who*, *Learners* was very low-tech and lacked intergalactic confrontation; its most violent scene involves Bev driving into a parked milk float. Nonetheless, as David explained, 'We've got a very specialised stunt team. The BBC are, as ever, very health and safety conscious – and quite right too, especially after *Top Gear*'s Richard Hammond took a bit of a tumble. Anything car-related is being particularly scrutinised.' Of course, this was not surprising at all at the time.

On 20 September 2006, Richard Hammond, one of Britain's most in-demand and best-loved television presenters, suffered a serious brain injury following a high-speed car crash. The nation held its breath while they watched the horror on television. A self-confessed daredevil and a petrolhead long before his association with *Top Gear*, it was while filming for the show, driving a jet-powered dragster at speeds of over 300mph that a tyre suddenly burst and the car speeded off the track and rolled over, burying the presenter. He was rescued, airlifted to hospital and hovered near death for several days until finally, he emerged from his coma. In recovery, he spent a year in which he felt lucid and plausible one moment, only to become confused, angry and exhausted the next. Despite this, he was lucky to have survived.

David himself didn't drive anything quite so fast. He would rather settle for a Skoda, which has, of course, over the years become the butt end of many a comedian's joke. Unlike Hammond, he sees cars as a means of transport rather than objects of desire. Mind you, he says, 'I do have more speeding points than are entirely practical, but that's only because I'm up and down on the M4 to Cardiff a lot. They have draconian speeding fines. There'll have been some work going on three weeks previously, so there's one sign saying "You should be going at 50 miles an hour here" and then 18 cameras to make sure that when inevitably you don't, with nobody else on the road at 3 a.m., they can charge you hundreds and hundreds of pounds for the privilege, but listen, I've just got far too many speeding points. What can I do to defend myself? It's my fault.'

But he was thrilled to have appeared in *Learners* because he hoped it would help to change the public's perception that he is a heartthrob. He told one journalist that the geeky driving instructor he plays would settle once and for all the question of his 'Sexiest Man Alive' tag. 'It was time to set the record straight,' he joked. 'I'd made a couple of deeply inaccurate appearances in some of those

"Sexy Men" charts, but nothing could be further from the truth and this film should help to right that wrong forever!'

Describing his character, Chris, as 'Not the sexiest article in the world', David admitted that his wardrobe in the show wasn't exactly high fashion either. 'What he wears isn't geek chic – it's just geek,' he laughed. 'Suits and trainers is geek chic, but not milk-bottle glasses and a haircut from 1964. He's not someone who ever considers what he looks like.'

But the main reason he accepted the role was because it meant that he would have another opportunity to work with Jessica Haynes. The two had worked together on the *Doctor Who* episodes, 'The Family of Blood' and 'Human Nature', in which she played potential companion Joan Redfern. When the opportunity came up again in *Learners*, David jumped at the opportunity: [When she was on the *Doctor Who* set], 'she told me she had this thing coming up, so I asked her if there was anything for me, and she thought I was joking, which I wasn't. So I kept asking and she told me there might be, and that was it. She's one of those actors who is so in the moment each time, in every scene, that she never fails to inspire you,' he raved. 'I've always been a fan of Jessica and when I worked with her, I became even more of a fan.'

The month after filming on *Learners* wrapped, David began work on yet another BBC drama. With *Lord of the Rings*' star Andy Serkis, Jim Broadbent, Lucy Cohu, Rebecca Hall and Jodhi May, he headed out to Hungary to film *Einstein and Eddington*, Peter Moffit's chronicle of the lives of the two men behind Albert Einstein's general theory of relativity during World War I, who refused to accept narrow nationalistic boundaries and continued to strive for a greater truth against the odds. Between them, they managed to change the world and proved one of the biggest scientific breakthroughs of the twentieth-century.

The drama, made by Company Pictures (the production company who also made Channel 4's *Shameless*), described how Albert Einstein and Eddington forged a relationship that ultimately brought worldwide acclaim for Einstein. Eddington's wholehearted belief that 'truth knows no boundaries' led him to start a correspondence with Einstein and to champion his theory at a time when the British rejected anything that was German. When Eddington goes to Africa to photograph light bending around the sun during an eclipse, Einstein's theory is proved to be correct, and this, in turn, transforms him into one of the most prominent and important astrophysicists of his time. Eventually he became a director of the Cambridge Observatory, a seat originally held by the father of British science, Sir Isaac Newton.

Along with Albert Einstein, Sir Arthur Eddington was one of the first physicists to understand the early ideas of relativity. Born on 28 December 1882 in Kendal, England, he never had an opportunity to know his father, who died when he was about two years old. Throughout his life, he kept to his Quaker beliefs, refusing to take part in active conflicts (including World War I). During his academic life, he was awarded several scholarships and he attended Owens College in Manchester, where he studied in the fields of physics and mathematics, graduating in 1902.

In 1907 he was awarded a fellowship to Trinity College and was named winner of a Smith's Prize for his various accomplishments in research into theoretical Physics, and Mathematics. From 1906–13, he was the primary assistant at the Greenwich Royal Observatory and then a professorship of astronomy at Cambridge. In 1914, he became a full member of the Royal Society and while at Cambridge, between 1914 and 1918, he became more knowledgeable in the area of relativity. The fact remains that for approximately a decade he and Einstein were the only people to have a full understanding of relativity.

In 1930, he was knighted Sir Arthur Eddington and went on to spend a large part of his remaining years critiquing the work of his colleagues in astrophysics. His most famous battle was over the constitution of white dwarf stars, when he heavily criticised the work of Subrahmanyan Chandrasekhar, although by this time his own ideas were outdated and incorrect. Other physicists silently backed Chandrasekhar, but refused to publicly discredit the great Eddington, who died on 22 November 1944 in Cambridge, England.

Eddington made significant contributions to general relativity and astrophysics, and can be regarded as the Father of Modern Theoretical Astrophysics. He published several books, including *Mathematical Theory of Relativity* in 1923, which Einstein referred to as the best publication in this area. In addition, he studied the properties of a solar eclipse on various expeditions around the world. His research eventually confirmed Einstein's theory that as light passes a massive star, its path is bent due to gravity.

Eddington spent a great amount of time researching the internal make up of stars. One of his findings was that the scattering of electrons is the primary source for the opacity of stars. He also determined that a star's luminosity is finite for a supplied mass. The divisor of the inequality for finding a star's maximum luminosity is now called the Eddington Limit, currently used in research on finding the sources of x-rays and black hole characteristics. The findings were published in 1926, in his book, *The Internal Constitution of Stars*.

Both Eddington and Einstein created arguments against the existence of black holes, which were subsequently disproved in the 1950s. As previously stated, Eddington also dismissed Chandrasekhar's theory of an upper limit for the mass of a white dwarf star, but his argument was incorrect and the Chandrasekhar Limit for the mass of a white dwarf remains the correct way to determine the upper bound for the mass of a white dwarf. Despite some mistakes and hostility to the views of some of his colleagues in later life, Arthur Eddington was a brilliant physicist, who made a significant contribution to science.

In the same year that David filmed scenes for *Einstein and Eddington*, he won the National Television Award for Most Popular Actor. In fact, the BBC had such confidence in him that they allowed him time off to play Hamlet, a commitment that ruled out a *Doctor Who* series for 2009. Instead, there are to be three bank holiday Specials spread over the year, with a fifth full series reaching screens in 2010, to which he is already informally committed.

'I think it's genuinely exciting that he's playing Hamlet,' said *Doctor Who* chief writer and executive producer, Russell T. Davies. 'I keep asking him what he's going to do with it and he doesn't know yet. He hasn't had time to concentrate, but it's a brilliant bit of casting. You'll get people in that theatre who would never normally go and watch *Hamlet* at the RSC. There'll be kids there who, in sixty years' time, will remember when they saw their first *Hamlet*.'

Interestingly enough, Hamlet, one of Shakespeare's great tragedies of a young man haunted by his father's ghost and driven to the edge of madness in his obsession to avenge his death, was another role that David has always wanted to play. Above all else, he was thrilled to be returning to the RSC to play the title role, directed by RSC Chief Associate Director Gregory Doran, who according to Nick Curtis, writing in the *Evening Standard*, must have been hugging himself.

Indeed, Doran was understandably over the moon that David had agreed to play the part and that the BBC had given him time off to do so. As he explained, 'It is a play that waits for the right actor to come along; it is a self-defining role. The Hamlet will be, to some extent who David is. At the same time, you have to have an actor who can be, as Ophelia describes him, "The poet, the soldier, the scholar." You have to have someone who is all those things, someone who is charismatic and can be brutal and coarse, and can be witty, and moving, and can physically take on the demands of the part, not just the fighting, but the sheer length of the role. It's the longest role in Shakespeare. And it needs someone who can give you something of those prismatic colours that the role contains.'

He continues: 'Hamlet is both fatalistic and aspirational. He is both forlorn and melancholy and very witty, and there are parts of the role that David will play with great ease. His skills with language are exceptional. It might be that there are areas of his melancholy and his reflection that David may have to tackle. David has great intelligence to tackle this role. It feels that there is no such thing as a definitive Hamlet – there are only an infinitive number of Hamlets. What I think he will get is the excitement of the role, the drive – Hamlet's experience of grief, his experience of what it is to grow up. All those things, I think he will approach with a freshness.'

Indeed, continued Doran, 'Hamlet is set in a world which is oppressed by a sense of surveillance. There is a constant sense of people overhearing each other – like Polonius sending people to spy on his own son. There are constantly people hiding behind arrases [a tapestry used as a wall-hanging or hanging screen] or leaving the stage in order to hear what's going on. It doesn't take long for Hamlet to discover that his old school friends have been sent to spy on him; that world of surveillance has clearly a sense of the contemporary. You sense that there is a danger that there is no privacy anymore. I think Hamlet as a play conveys something of that paranoia.

'I think it will be defined by the actors who are in it. Patrick Stewart has been in it numerous times for this company, playing different roles. He will play Claudius and the ghost. When I was talking to Patrick, I quickly realised that you mustn't view Claudius through Hamlet's point of view; he is trying to sort out the kingdom. It might not be a completely selfless agenda, but it could be that the old King Hamlet was not a good King. It could be that in order to find stability for the kingdom he has also basically leapt over Hamlet's own right to run things because he thinks that Hamlet would be a dreadful mess. I don't think that Hamlet shows a lot of evidence of leadership skills and we might need people like Claudius sometimes.'

Having worked with David before, Doran considered him unlikely to be deterred by any of the previous portrayals of the role. The early 1960s, for example, witnessed a slew of actors in the role: Ian Bannen, Richard Burton, David Warner, and of course, David's old *Casanova* ally, Peter O'Toole, to name but a few. In his opinion, Mark Rylance's near-definitive performance (back in 1989) was unfairly eclipsed by the breakdown suffered by Daniel Day-Lewis while playing the same part at the National. He had reportedly seen his own dead father, the poet laureate Cecil Day-Lewis, as the ghost of Hamlet's father.

Of all the parts, says Doran, since it was first performed in the 1600s, 'it's been going on somewhere in the world ever since. There's been an unbroken line from Richard Burbage right through to David Tennant. Even through the closure of the theatres in 1642, you can trace the line. Richard Burbage, we know, handed it on to Joseph Taylor [his apprentice and understudy]. We know that William Davenant saw Taylor play the role and taught it to Betterton when he took over the role and the restoration. And then right through to Garrick to Kean, Irving, Gielgud, Olivier, Branagh, there is this unbroken line of people experiencing Hamlet, and in this particular company since 1879 after the Shakespeare Memorial Theatre was built, *Hamlet* has never been far from the repertoire.'

To begin with, he was anxious about directing *Hamlet*, but as the opening at the Courtyard Theatre in Stratford-upon-Avon approached in July 2008, it was more of a nervous excitement, as he describes it: 'I've now done half the canon for the RSC and *Hamlet* is one that I don't think I've avoided, but I just haven't known how to tackle it. Now we have a cast and creative team in place, it feels less daunting than it did. Once you've determined there isn't such a thing as a definitive *Hamlet*, you can only do it with an open heart and a mind that is open to the rest of the world. As Hamlet says, "It holds a mirror up to nature."'

After Doran watched David on tracing-your-roots programme *Who Do You Think You Are* in September 2006, he sent him a text that same night, saying that he had just seen his audition for *Hamlet* and asked outright if he had ever thought about playing Hamlet. 'He said that the two roles he really wanted to do were Hamlet and Berowne in *Love's Labours Lost*. I had already decided that I would be directing *Love's Labours Lost* as it had been 15 years since we'd done it and thought it was an extraordinary coincidence. It all came together in a perfect flash of coincidence and synergy. There was a long time where we had to keep it under our hats whilst the BBC sorted out his temporary vacation of the Tardis.'

Once it was all finalised, David ruefully admitted how scared he was: 'It doesn't feel right somehow to know that I'll be doing a matinée of *Hamlet* on some afternoon in 18 months' time. It's lovely, but it's also absurd. Seeing the dates printed in black and white in the RSC schedule makes me feel terrified, a whole year in advance; it's a fear on a daily basis.'

But it wasn't just nerves that concerned him. David also found himself the victim of a stalker: a woman who had moved to Stratford-upon-Avon, rented a flat directly opposite the Courtyard Theatre, and started to hassle cast members of the production by telling them that she had left her husband for David, regularly left pencil drawings for him of them being friendly in the Tardis, as well as bizarre sci-fi versions of *Hamlet*, featuring herself as Ophelia and David as a futuristic Hamlet. According to the *Daily Star* in January 2008, she was even insisting that both the Doctor and Hamlet are aliens in a hostile universe, terrified of being alone. What made matters worse was the news that she had bought front-row tickets for the production every weekend until it finished in November. 'It's all a bit unnerving,' said one source. 'He won't be able to spot her in the audience because he doesn't know what she looks like.' David's only protection was to carry on with business as normal.

By the time he had started rehearsals, he had just completed filming another *Doctor Who* Christmas Special, and his third series had already started its run on BBC. It followed the familiar pattern of previous outings since the show had been so successfully re-launched by writer-producer Russell T. Davies in 2005. The Doctor's latest adventures were as ever under wraps; the plot twists and turns shrouded in secrecy in similar style to a new Harry Potter novel. All that was known as the first episode hit the screen in April 2008 was that Catherine Tate would be playing his new assistant.

'In this series we've pushed the Doctor further than he's ever gone before,' said Davies. 'I've made 39 episodes with David now, and I'm still going; he's just limitless. Sometimes you find yourself writing for actors and allowing for their traits. There's nothing worse than sitting at your desk at two in the morning thinking, I can't have them cry in this scene because they're no good at crying, which you find with actors sometimes.'

But, as he continues, 'there's none of that with David. You can watch him in *Doctor Who*, and then in a serious drama like *Recovery* and it's like you're watching a different man. In *Harry Potter and the Goblet of Fire* he has a small part, but it's a perfect little distillation of evil. You can write anything for him; you're never bored and you never want him to have bad lines of dialogue – you want to do your best for him.'

All the same, it transpired that it was the last *Doctor Who* series that Davies had written for him. In May 2008, as David was in rehearsal for *Hamlet*, he stepped down from his role as lead writer and executive producer and handed over to BAFTA-winning writer Steven Moffat to do the writing and producing honours for the fifth series.

BBC fiction controller Jane Tranter said the past four series of *Doctor Who* had been brilliantly helmed by the 'spectacularly talented' Davies: 'As lead writer and executive producer, he has overseen the creative direction and detail of the twenty-first century re-launch of *Doctor Who* and we are delighted to have his continued presence on the Specials over the next 18 months.' Indeed Davies would remain in charge of four Specials to be shown in 2009: 'I love *Doctor Who* and I love the old *Doctor Who*, but even with all that love, you have to admit that the name of the programme and its reputation had become a joke … you know, rubber monsters and shaky sets. It's been everything we planned and more, and it's very rarely in life you get the chance to have that happen.'

Like Davies, David too has a thoroughly congenial reputation – and not just among luvvies. Newspaper diarists, who often find themselves at the sharp end of a dressing-down from a celebrity, say he's the perfect gentleman, always polite and ready to talk when cornered at a media event. He's one of the few public figures approved by celebrity and pop music gossip site *Popbitch*, which has posted more than one tale of the actor's loveliness and largesse. And Davies himself positively gushes with praise for his star: 'People can get tired and ratty on set, but David never does. There must be times when he feels low, but he feels the responsibility of leading the team. It's not his job to lead – as an actor he could be miserable as fuck if he wanted to be, but he's a proper leader of men.'

The gay newspaper, *The Pink Paper*, once granted David the title of 'Sexiest Man in the Universe,' but despite having played Casanova for the BBC, David's good looks are not of the movie-star variety: he is skinny and angular, with limbs that can flail with comic urgency as *Doctor Who* or crazed hostility, as they did when he played the deranged Barty Crouch Jr in *Harry Potter and the Goblet of Fire*. His tall, lean physiognomy will set him apart from the other notable Hamlets of recent years.

He won the role of Doctor Who after impressing Davies on the set of *Casanova* in 2005, but even his producer has been shocked by the resounding success of the show and its star: 'The show's success is so mad that I don't think any of us will get our heads round it till it's all over and we look back on it in ten years' time and say, "Blimey, that was weird!" But I think what the public like about David is his energy. He glitters on screen; there's a vitality to him that is undeniably what has worked with the Doctor. On set we're surrounded by props and monsters and explosions and things often go wrong. When they do, we say to each other, "Well, at least we've got David." We put the camera on him and it just comes to life.'

In the same month that David started his run of *Hamlet* at the Courtyard Theatre in Stratford-upon-Avon, trying to forget about the stalker that haunted him since he began rehearsals, and probably wondering how his relationship with Georgia Moffett would pan out, the boy who had grown up dreaming of being Doctor Who, was about to be seen on film in a special *Doctor Who* clip at the Proms during the *Doctor Who* night at the Royal Albert Hall that was hosted by Freema Agyeman and a procession of Daleks and Cybermen.

Neither could he help wondering about his future in *Doctor Who*. But as he had now fulfilled his childhood dream, perhaps he wasn't that worried. Answering speculation about whether he would return for the show's fifth season in 2010, David seemed unsure. He told Andrew Marr, in June 2008, that he had not then been asked and when he was he would consider the question. Even though he was committed to start filming four specials in January 2009 (when Jude Law would step into his *Hamlet* shoes as it moved into London's West End) to bridge the gap between the fourth season and the fifth, nothing had been firmed up for a new series.

Whether David is at the height of his career now or not, perhaps he is right to just go along with it. As he says, the highlight of any career should be wherever you are at the time. 'I certainly don't think the best is all behind me. I often stop when I'm doing something, in the middle of rehearsals or some other job, and I try to take a minute to think, "Okay, this might be as good as it gets, so drink it in, appreciate it now." So far, I've been lucky because another job has always come along to equal the last.'

And he concludes, 'You don't know where your life will go. I'd be amazed after all this time if one day I just thought I've had enough [of acting], but I guess life does change, doesn't it? Priorities change. It is quite a self-centred life, any kind of vocational life is, but I'd like to think I could go on forever. It's nice to be in a profession where there's a need for you at every stage of life.'

Today, his standing as a British cultural icon is completely secure. Jonathan Miller slated him in the press for taking on *Hamlet*, and indeed, West End theatres for putting celebrity ahead of quality, but one could hardly call Miller's outburst justified when it came to David. He has such a strong classical pedigree, including a first-rate RSC (Royal Shakespeare Company) Romeo, it makes Miller's criticism sound like sour grapes. After all, David is far more than just your average run-of-the-mill celebrity.

A poll conducted by the BBC in 2006 found that he was the nation's favourite Doctor Who of all-time, beating Jon Pertwee, Christopher Eccleston and even his own favourite, Tom Baker. One year after, when David was thirty-six, he came in at number 24 in a media power list, making him perhaps one of the most powerful actors in television. And now, having been named the Sexiest

Leading Man in television, with his reputation for being one of the nicest guys in showbiz that you could ever wish to meet, it is clear that, even though he keeps his private life very private, his public life could not be better.

GLOSSARY

BY CHARLOTTE RASMUSSEN

The following is a guide to some of the definitions frequently used in the technical and creative side of filmmaking, which readers may find useful as a glossary to this book:

AD LIB

From the Latin phrase *ad libitum*, meaning 'in accordance with desire', this is improvised dialogue where the actors make up what they say in real time on the movie set or on stage. When in the exact situation required by the script the actors (or the director) often discover that the production may benefit from a different dialogue or reaction. This way, the final result is often much improved.

AGENT

The manager responsible for the professional business dealings of an actor, director, screenwriter or other artist, an agent typically negotiates the contracts and often has some part in selecting or recommending roles for their client. Professional actors usually have assistants, publicists and other personnel in addition to this involved in handling their day-to-day schedule and career.

BILLING

The placement (or display) of names of actors, directors and producers for a movie in publicity materials, opening (or closing) film credits, and on theatre marquees. A person's status is indicated by the size, relative position and placement of their name. Generally, positions closer to the top, with larger and more prominent letters, designate higher importance and greater box-office draw, and precede people of lesser importance. The most prominent actor that appears first is said to have top billing, followed by second billing, and so forth.

BLOCKBUSTER

A movie that is a huge financial success: $100 million or more. The gross of a movie is, to some extent, a measure of the popularity and talent of its leading actors and can determine whether or not a sequel is economically worthwhile. Often the term gross profit is mentioned in reference to 'first dollar gross' and this form of compensation entitles an individual to a percentage of every dollar of gross receipts.

BLOCKING

The rehearsal used to determine the position and movement of the camera, actors and crew during a particular shot or scene.

BLOOPER

Funny outtakes and mistakes by cast or crew caught on camera. Bloopers are sometimes included in the end-credits of a movie or in the special features section of the final DVD, also known as blooper reels or gag reels. Causes for bloopers are often uncontrollable laughter, props (falling, breaking or failing to work as expected), forgotten lines or sudden incidents such as a bird flying in front of the camera. The term blooper is sometimes also applied to a continuity error, which somehow goes unnoticed (and makes it through) the editing process and is thus released in the final product for viewers to see. However, strictly speaking this is a film error, not a blooper.

BLUE SCREEN

Special effects photography in which a subject (an object or a performer) is photographed in front of a uniformly illuminated blue or green screen; during post-production, the coloured screen is optically or electronically eliminated and a new background substituted in its place, allowing images to be combined. Blue is normally used for people (because the human skin has very little blue colour to it) and green for digital shots (the green colour channel retains more detail and requires less light). Other colours may be used depending on what technique is applied. Often used to achieve the effect of a natural environment, such as a forest, beach, prairie, mountain or other landscape in a shot or sequence, but also to create science fiction worlds, or environments that are in-accessible during production.

BOOM POLE

Operated by a person from the sound department, the boom pole is a special piece of equipment. It is made from a length of light aluminium or carbon fibre that allows precise positioning of the microphone, above or below the actors, just out of the camera's frame.

BOX OFFICE

Measure of the total amount of money paid by moviegoers to see a movie in theatres.

B-ROLL

Cutaway shots used to cover the visual part of an interview or narration. Often made available on the Internet or on DVDs as extra material.

CALL BACK

The follow-up after an audition when the actor in question is called back for a more personal meeting, maybe to discuss the script or the character. It gives the director and producers a chance to consider whether the actor is appropriate for the role and to check if there is the necessary chemistry between other members of the cast.

CALL SHEET

The call sheet details what is being filmed on a particular day, in scene order. It lists the same information to be found in the liner shooting schedule, plus each character name, what extras are needed and what time each actor is to be picked up, when they are required to go into makeup/hair and onto set. Crew and special requirements for each scene are also noted.

CAMEO

Small part played by a famous actor, who would ordinarily not accept such an insignificant role for little, sometimes even no money. Often big Hollywood stars choose to appear in independent productions to support and perhaps draw attention to the specific movie (theme, co-star or director).

CAMERA DOLLY

The camera can be mounted on top of this little moveable car. During shooting it is often placed on tracks to ensure stability.

CAST

The characters physically present in the play or film. These are the roles for which actors will be needed.

CD

First generation of optical media with a storage capacity of up to 700 MB, mostly used for music, data and images, but some CDs are designed specifically for video (such as VCD or SVCD).

CGI

Computer Generated Image: A term denoting computers have been used to generate the full imagery.

CHARACTER

Any personified entity appearing in a film or a play.

COMPOSITE VIDEO

The format of analogue television before combined with audio, composed by three signals called Y (luminance), U and V (both carrying colour information).

CREDITS

The opening credit is an on-screen text that describes the most important people involved in the making of a movie. End credit is usually a rolling list at the end of the movie, where everybody involved (cast, crew, studio, producers etc.) is named or thanked.

CUTTING ROOM

Location where film rolls or tapes are edited by cutting out the unwanted parts.

DAILIES

First positive prints made from the negatives photographed on the previous day. Watching the dailies often determines which scenes needs to be re-shot or changed.

DIRECTOR

In a stage play, the individual responsible for staging (placing in the space or blocking) the actors, sculpting and coordinating their performances, and ensuring they fit with the design elements into a coherent vision of the play. In a musical, there will typically be a separate musical director responsible for the musical elements of the show. In a Dramatists Guild contract, the playwright has approval over the choice of director (and the cast and designers). In film, however, the director carries out the duties of a stage director and has considerably more say-so over the final product. A casting director plays an important part of pre-production in selecting the cast. This usually involves auditions and if hundreds or thousands of candidates come in to perform, special staff are required to be in charge of this process.

DISTRIBUTOR

Organisation responsible for coordinating the distribution of the finished movie to exhibitors, as well as the sale of videos, DVDs, laserdiscs and other media versions of movies.

DUBBING

Dubbing or looping is the process of recording voices to match the exact mouth-movements of the actors on screen. Often used to replace the original language with another (i.e. Spanish voice track over an American movie). Dubbing or ADR (Additional Dialogue Recording or post-synchronisation) is also used to re-record the lines by the same actor, who originally spoke them – often the case when the original sound on set was interrupted by unwanted or uncontrollable noise such as traffic or is just too un-clear. The actors are then called into a sound studio. While watching the film on video they re-perform their line, which is recorded by a sound technician.

DVD

Short for Digital Versatile Disc or Digital Video Disc. Like a CD, a DVD is an optical media, but has much higher density. There are many different types of DVDs (DVD-R, DVD+R, DVD, DVD-RW, DVD+RW) and they are used for video, audio and data storage. Most DVDs used for movies are 12cm in diameter and their usual sizes are 4.7 GB (single layer) or 8.5 GB (dual layer) – both types can be double-sided. Dual layer DVDs have a semi-transparent layer on top, in which the red laser shines through to reach the layer at the bottom. Switching from one layer to another may cause a noticeable pause in some DVD players. A newer type of high-density disc is the High Definition DVD (HD DVD), which is able to store three times as much data as the standard DVD format. The Blu-ray disc (BD) offers storage capacity up to 25 GB (single layer). Blu-ray format uses a blue-violet laser (with a shorter wavelength than the typical red laser), which enables a Blu-ray disc to be packed more tightly.

EXTRAS

Individuals who appear in a movie where a non-specific, non-speaking character is required, usually as part of a crowd or in the background of a scene. Often family-members of the cast or crew (who may hang around the set anyway) are used.

FEATURE FILM

A movie primarily for distribution in theatres, it is at least 60 minutes long or the script at least 90 pages long. As opposed to feature films, these are movies made for TV or produced for video-release only.

FOLEY

The art of recreating incidental sound effects (such as footsteps) in synchronisation with the visual component of a movie.

FRAME

Movies are created by taking a rapid sequence of pictures (frames) of action and by displaying these frames at the same rate at which they were recorded, thus creating an illusion of motion. In the US, film equals 24 frames per second (NTSC) and video equals 30 frames per second (NTSC). In Europe, most film equals 25 frames per second (PAL). In France and fractions of Europe, Africa and the former USSR, another standard called SECAM is used.

FRANCHISE

A media franchise (literature, film, videogame, TV programme) is a property involving characters, settings, trademarks, etc. Media franchises tend to cross over from their original media to other forms (i.e. from books to films). Generally a whole series is made in a particular medium, along with merchandise. Some franchises are planned in advance, others happen by accident because of a sudden profitable success.

FREEBIE

Promotional samples such as tickets, clothing, gadgets,

promotional DVDs, books or whatever the production or distributing company chooses to give away free of charge, maybe in limited amounts. Some may be signed by the cast or are otherwise unique merchandise or bonus material.

GATE

The film gate is an opening in front of the camera where the film is exposed to light. Sometimes the film celluloid can break off, giving débris known as hair that can create a dark line on the edge of the film frame. Such a hair can only be removed by painting it out digitally in post-production, an annoying, time-consuming and costly affair. Several factors influence the frequency of hairs: environment, humidity, camera position, type of film, etc. When the director feels he has got a particular shot he calls out to the crew to 'check the gate'; a clean shot is replied with 'gate is good'. Note: this problem does not exist when shooting digitally.

GRIP

A trained lighting and rigging technician.

HOOK

A term borrowed from song-writing and used to describe a thing (or line) that catches the public's attention and keeps them interested in the flow of a story.

INDEPENDENT FILMS

Also known as 'Indies', these films are financed by a smaller production company independent of a major film studio. Often they produce small, interesting movies on a low budget, which sometimes get no further than recognition at film festivals and/or are released in a limited number of theatres.

LASERDISC

First type of commercial optical disc (LD) with a common size of 30cm in diameter. 18 and 12 cm discs were also published. Analogue video combined with digital audio. Laserdiscs were recorded in three different formats: CAV, CLV and CAA. Mostly caught on in North America and Japan, only to be quickly replaced by the more popular and smaller DVDs when they were introduced.

LOCATION

The physical site where all or part of a film is produced as opposed to the set or soundstage. If the storyline is based on authentic events, it doesn't necessarily mean the exact same location where the action took place in real life but something similar.

METHOD ACTING

Sometimes referred to as 'the method', it is a style of acting formalised by Russian actor and theatre director Konstantin Stanislavsky. The actor interprets the role by drawing from experiences in his own personal life in direct parallel to the character.

MINIATURES

Small landscapes, towns or buildings built in miniature (and usually to scale) to make effects that are impossible to achieve otherwise, either because it is too expensive or too dangerous to do so in reality.

OPTION

Legal agreement to rent the rights to a script for a specific period of time.

PADDING

Material added to clothing or shoes to enhance an actor's physical appearance or to protect a stuntman from unnecessary injuries.

PLOT

The order of events in a story: the main plot is called A-plot. Typical plot structure includes (a) Beginning/initial situation, (b) Conflict/problem which has to be achieved/solved, (c) Complications to overcome, (d) Climax, (e) Suspense, (f) Resolution (or not) after the conflict/problem has been solved and (g) Conclusion/end. Simplified, a dramatic structure of a story can be divided into five acts: exposition, rising action, climax (turning point), falling action and resolution (dénouement), meaning unravelling or untying of the plot). This is also known as Freytag's pyramid.

PRODUCER

The person or entity financially responsible for a stage or film production; the chief of a movie production in all matters save the creative efforts of the director, who raises funding, hires key personnel, and arranges distribution. An executive producer is not involved in any technical aspects of the filmmaking process, but is still responsible for the overall production (usually handling business and legal issues). The production company is headed up by a producer, director, actor or writer and is to create general entertainment products such as motion pictures, television shows, infomercials, commercials and multimedia.

PRODUCTION

Pre-production is the stage during the creation of the movie where the producer gets everything ready to shoot: hiring actors through casting, picking directors and the rest of the crew, making costumes, finding locations, editing the script, constructing sets, doing rehearsals, etc. The production is the actual shooting of the movie (also known as principal photography). In post-production (or simply post), extra scenes or alternative versions are shot. Also includes editing and cutting of the movie, creating CGI special effects, adding sound-effects and composing the music score and generally making promotion (press-conferences, trailer shows, billboards, etc.) before the première.

PROP

A prop is any object held, manipulated or carried by a performer during a theatrical performance, on stage or film. For example, stage gun, mock glassware, etc.

RATING

In the USA, The Motion Picture Association of America (MPAA) and the National Association of Theatre Owners (NATO) operate a rating system for movies: G (general audience, all ages admitted), PG (parental guidance suggested, some material may not be suitable for children), PG-13 (parents strongly cautioned, some material may be inappropriate for children under 13), R (restricted, under 17, requires accompanying parent or adult guardian) and NC-17 (no one 17 and under will be admitted). The rating for a particular movie is decided by a board of parents. They also define an informational warning for the particular movie, along with the rating (i.e. for strong language, violence, nudity, drug abuse, etc.). In the UK, the British Board of Film Classification (BBFC) classifies films and videos. The rating system differs from the American system: U (suitable for audiences aged 4 years and over, while movies classified Uc are particularly suitable for pre-school children), PG (general viewing, but some scenes may be unsuitable for young children), 12 (no one younger than 12 may rent or buy the movie; movies classified 12A may not be seen by children younger than 12 in the cinema unless accompanied by an adult), 15 (suitable only for 15 years and over; no one younger may buy, rent or see a movie in a cinema), 18 (suitable only for adults; no one younger may buy, rent or see a movie in a cinema). Movies classified R18 mean a special and legally restricted classification, they are to be shown only in specially licensed cinemas and may only be supplied in licensed shops, never by mail order.

RED CARPET

A red carpet is a strip of carpet in the colour red, laid out in front of a building to welcome VIPs such as dignitaries and celebrities to formal events such as premières, special screenings, press conferences, etc.

REGION ENCODING

To avoid the newest movie released in the United States on DVD from being played in other parts of the world before they have even premièred in theatres there, a DVD region locking system is used to control which type of DVDs can be played on DVD players. DVDs are coded for 9 different regions (0–8) and they require a DVD player of the same region to play the DVD. The Blu-ray movie region codes are different from DVDs and there are currently three: A/1, B/2, C/3.

REHEARSAL

Preparatory event in music and theatre, this is a form of practice to ensure professionalism and to eliminate mistakes by working on details without performing in public or on camera. At a dress rehearsal the ensemble tries out their wardrobe for the first time and the different outfits and costumes are fitted to match their exact size.

RE-SHOOT

When it is clear that some scenes don't fit each other very well or the story doesn't come together as intended, it is sometimes necessary to shoot a scene again after principal photography has ended. It may be months after the final wrap when the actors are called back to re-shoot their part.

SCENE

Continuous block of storytelling, set in a single location or following a particular character.

SCORE

Any printed version of a musical arrangement for opera, film or other musical work in notational form, it may include lyrics or supplemental text.

SCREENING

The showing of a film for test audiences and/or people involved in the making of the movie, often several different cuts of a movie are produced in the process. This is why a DVD sometimes refers to the term 'director's cut' whereas the final version that hits the theatres is a collaboration between the director, editors, producers and the studio executives.

SCRIPT

Blueprint or roadmap outlining a movie story through visual descriptions, actions of characters and their dialogue, a lined script is a copy of the shooting script prepared by the script supervisor during production to indicate (via notations and vertical lines drawn directly onto the script pages) exactly what coverage has been shot. The production script is the script prepared and ready to be put into production. A shooting script has changes known as revised pages made to the production script after the initial circulation. These pages are different in colour and incorporated into the shooting script without displacing or rearranging the original, unrevised pages. A method of script submission in which the writer sends the script (without prior contact) to the theatre or production company is called an unsolicited script.

SEQUEL

A second creative work (book, movie, play) set in the same universe as the first, but later in time. Often employs elements such as characters, settings or plots as the original story. Opposed to prequel that is set before the original story. Prequels suffer the disadvantage of the audience knowing what the outcome will be.

SET

The physical elements constructed or arranged to create a sense of place. Usually there is a set designer/art director, as well as other professional designers whose job it is to envision any of the following elements: costumes, sets, lights, sounds or properties.

SITCOM

Also known as a situation comedy. In the US it is normally a 30-minute comedic television show revolving around funny situations for the main characters.

SOAP OPERA

Daytime drama. So-called because it airs during the day and was originally sponsored by the makers of laundry detergent in the early days of television.

SOUNDSTAGE

Large studio area where elaborate sets may be constructed and usually a sound-proof, hangar-like building.

SPOILER

A summary or description relating plot elements not revealed early in the narrative itself. Moreover, because enjoyment of a narrative sometimes depends upon the dramatic tension and suspense, this early revelation of plot elements can 'spoil' the enjoyment otherwise experienced. The term spoiler is often associated with special Internet sites and in newsgroup postings. Usually, the spoiling information is preceded by a warning.

STILLS

Static photographs taken from a movie and usually used for advertising purposes.

STORYBOARD

An organised set of graphics used to illustrate and visualise the sequence of filming. Looks like a comic and is used early in the filming process to experiment and move scenes around. Newer movie-makers often prefer computerised animations.

STUNTS

Trained and professional stunt personnel used in dangerous situations to avoid exposing the cast to any risk or for acts requiring special skills (for instance, diving, falling or a car crash). The stunt is carried out by the actor's stunt double, which is not to be confused with a body/photo double (a look-alike used for scenes where the actor isn't required, i.e. shots where the face isn't visible or for scenes involving nudity).

SUBTITLES

Also known as Closed Captions (CC). 'Closed' meaning they are only visible when activated (i.e. extra features on a DVD) as opposed to 'open' captioning, where all viewers see the captions all the time (i.e. TV programmes). They are used in the following ways: (i) explanatory when foreign languages are used in a movie, (ii) for hearing impaired and (iii) as general translation for viewers not speaking the language in question.

SYNDICATION

The sale of the right to broadcast radio shows and television shows to multiple individual stations, without going through a broadcast network. It is common in countries where television is organized around networks with local affiliates, notably the United States. Shows can also be syndicated internationally.

TABLE-READ

When the writer (or writing team) is finished with the script, it's time for the table-read. During this process the entire cast of actors, all the writers, producers and anyone else who is interested, gets together and acts out the script. This is very important because it lets the writers finally hear how their words sound spoken out loud. They pay close attention to the audience's reaction and take notes on what works and what doesn't – for example, do people get the jokes and laugh at the right places? Afterwards, the writers (and sometimes producers) discuss the problems and explore ways to improve the script.

TAPE MARKS

Most times the exact spot where the actors are supposed to be standing is marked with tape on the floor (off-camera), since it's important for the cameraman and the rest of the cast to know where everyone is positioned.

TEASER/TRAILER

A set of scenes used for promotional purposes, appearing on television and in theatres before other films is called a teaser since it is used to 'tease' the audience and grab their attention. Like the teaser, the trailer is a short, edited montage of selected scenes to be used as an advertisement for the film, a preview of coming attractions. Running times vary from 15 seconds to 3 minutes. Not everything in the trailer will necessarily appear in the final film since the trailer is often produced early in the filming process. A trailer is sometimes used as a selling tool to raise funds for a feature film. Originally it was shown at the end of a film (hence the term 'trailer'), but people left the theatre before seeing it and so it was moved to the beginning.

TRAILER

A mobile home for the actors while filming on location or in a studio, it can be a mid-sized RV (recreational vehicle). The trailers may be elaborately equipped with bedroom, bathroom, small kitchen, etc. since the actors sometimes spend a lot of hours there, preparing their work, having meetings, relaxing, spending time with their family or just hanging out and waiting in-between takes. Some trailers are made into schoolrooms, dressing rooms or hair and make-up trailers, where the cast is fixed up before the shoot. For temporary stays, such as on a movie-set, the trailers do not become so personalised as for larger productions, such as on-going television shows where the actors tend to decorate their home-away-from-home.

TWO-SHOT

Close-up camera shot of two people in the foreground, framed from the chest up, and often in dialogue with each other to indicate relationship information. Likewise three-shot, etc.

VHS

The Video Home System is a recording and playing standard for analogue video-cassette recorders (VCR). The recording medium is magnetic tape. Several variations exist (VHS-C, Super-VHS and others), each again dependent on the type of signal (SECAM, PAL or NTSC).

VOICE OVER

Also known as V.O. or off-camera commentary, a speaker narrates the action onscreen.

WIDE-ANGLE SHOT

A shot filmed with a lens that is able to take in a wider field of view (to capture more of the scene's elements or objects) than a regular lens.

WIDESCREEN

Refers to projection systems in which the aspect ratio is wider than the 1.33:1 ratio, which dominated sound film before the 1950s. In the 1950s, many widescreen processes were introduced to combat the growing popularity of television, such as CinemaScope (an anamorphic system), VistaVision (non-anamorphic production technique in which the film is run horizontally through the camera instead of vertically), and Todd-AO and Super Panavision (both used wider-gauge film). Also known as letterboxing.

WRAP

Term used to define the end of shooting, either for the day or the entire production, and short for Wind Roll And Print. Often associated with the wrap party, where cast, crew, producers, studio executives and other associates get together on the last day of filming to celebrate.

FILMOGRAPHY

FEATURE FILMS

1996

Jude – Directed by Michael Winterbottom. David's film debut in a drama about a stonemason who steadfastly pursues a cousin he loves. Adapted from the Thomas Hardy novel of the same name, his co-stars included a youthful Kate Winslet and another future Doctor Who, Christopher Eccleston.

1997

Bite – Directed by Brian Ross. David plays Alistair Galbraith, a postman who is splitting up with his cheating wife. The only living thing that seems to take an interest in him is a huge great German Shepherd he encounters on his round.

1998

LA Without A Map – Directed by Mika Kaurismaki. David plays Richard, who has his life turned upside down during a burial in a Bradford cemetery, when he meets Barbara, a beautiful young actress from Los Angeles.

1999

The Last September – Directed by Deborah Warner. David plays Captain Gerald Colthurst, who romantically frolics with Keeley Hawes in a film about the demise of a family, who see in the end of an era and a way of life with which they have become familiar.

2000

Being Considered – Directed by Jonathan Newman. British comedy about a struggling artist and filmmaker who can't quite keep life together in the face of other people's success.

2001

Sweetnightgoodheart – Directed by Dan Zeff. Another of David's short comedy films, in which he plays Pete, who starts to break up with girlfriend Kate Ashfield on the phone and gets interrupted. Kate thinks he's proposing, and he ends up with a house full of well-wishing friends and family.

FILMOGRAPHY

2002

Nine and Half Minutes – Directed by Josh Appignanesi and Misha Manson-Smith. David and Zoe Telford play a couple who meet on a blind date and go from introduction, seduction and relationship to boredom and break-up – in nine and half minutes.

2003

Bright Young Things – Directed by Stephen Fry. Adapted from a Evelyn Waugh novel, David plays Ginger Littlejohn in a comedy-drama set in the 1930s about a host of young people who beautified London nightclubs, dancing and jazz.

2004

Old Street – Directed by Angus Jackson.

Traffic Warden – Directed by Donald Rice. David is a traffic warden in a short film about a beautiful girl, a bowl of goldfish and an illegally parked car.

2005

Harry Potter and the Goblet of Fire – Directed by Mike Newell. Based on JK Rowling's bestselling children's book, this was the first of David's breakthrough roles to bring him to the attention of the public when he played Barty Crouch Jr in the fourth instalment about the schoolboy wizard.

2006

Free Jimmy – Directed by Christopher Nielsen. An animated film about four stoners, five vegans, three mobsters, four hunters and a million reasons to free one junkie elephant, in which David provides the voice for a character named Hamish.

TELEVISION

1994

Takin' Over The Asylum – Directed by David Blair. David played Campbell McBain, a manic depressive, in a series about a group of patients at a Scottish mental hospital.

1998

Duck Patrol – Directed by Sylvie Boden. A comedy series about PC Simon 'Darwin' Brown, played by David, which follows the activities of the officers of the Ravensbeck River Police Station.

2004

The Traffic Warden – Directed by Donald Rice. David played Chris in a one-off comedy drama about learner drivers.

He Knew He Was Right – Directed by Tom Vaughan. In this three-part mini series, David played the Revd. Gibson in an adaptation of the Anthony Trollope classic.

FILMOGRAPHY

Blackpool – Directed by Julie Anne Robinson. David played DI Peter Carlisle in a six-part musical murder-mystery set in Blackpool.

2005

Casanova – Directed by Sheeree Folkson. Written by *Doctor Who* writer Russell T. Davies, this was the role that would eventually lead to David landing the part of the Doctor. In this three-part series based on the life and loves of Casanova, he played the title role.

The Quatermass Experiment – Directed by Sam Miller. David played Dr Gordon Briscoe in a one-off live performance of the classic sci-fi show.

Secret Smile – Directed by Christopher Menaul. David played Brendan Block in a two-part dramatisation of the Nicci French novel of the same name.

Doctor Who: 'The Christmas Invasion'. Directed by James Hawes. David's first outing as the Doctor but he spends most of the episode in bed recovering from the draining regeneration process, while Billie Piper as Rose battles sinister masked Santas, a killer Christmas tree and a plot to take over the world by the Sycorax, a monstrous alien race.

2006

The Romantics – Directed by Sam Hobkinson. Played Jean-Jacques Rousseau in a series charting the careers of a group of writers known as The Romantics.

Doctor Who Series 2 – Various directors. David's first series as the Doctor with Billie Piper as his companion, Rose Tyler.

The Chatterley Affair – Directed by James Hawes. Played Richard Hoggart in a dramatisation of the sensational 1960s literary trial.

Recovery – Directed by Andy DeEmmony. Played Alan Hamilton in a one-off drama about a man coping with a brain injury.

Doctor Who: 'The Runaway Bride' – Directed by Euros Lyn. David's second Christmas Special as the Doctor, with Catherine Tate as Donna, a bride who finds herself aboard the Tardis on the eve of her wedding. The Doctor must discover her connection with the Empress of Racnoss's plan to destroy the world.

2007

Doctor Who Series 3 – Directed by various. David played the Doctor for his second series, and is joined by Freema Agyeman as his companion, Martha Jones.

Doctor Who: 'Voyage of the Damned' – directed by James Strong. David teamed up with Kylie Minogue for a feature-length Christmas Special that became the most-watched *Doctor Who* episode in history. After the *Titanic* collides with the Tardis, David and Kylie battle aliens, saboteurs and robot angels.

2008

Einstein and Eddington – Directed by Philip Martin. Played Sir Arthur Eddington in a one-off drama about the relationship between Albert Einstein and British physicist Sir Arthur Eddington.

Doctor Who Series 4 – directed by various. For the third series with David as the Doctor, he was reunited with Catherine Tate's Donna from the 2006 Christmas Special.

THEATRE

1995

What The Butler Saw

1996

As You Like It
The General From America
The Herbal Bed
Vassa

1997

Hurly Burly

1998

Black Comedy
The Real Inspector Hound

1999

An Experienced Woman Gives Advice
King Lear

2000

The Comedy of Errors
The Rivals
Twelve Angry Men

2001

Comedians
Slab Boys Trilogy

2002

Hay Fever
Lobby Hero
Long's Day's Journey Into Night
Push Up
Romeo & Juliet
Tartuffe

FILMOGRAPHY

The Glass Menagerie
Who's Afraid of Virginia Woolf?

2003
The Pillowman

2005
Look Back In Anger
Merlin

2008
Love's Labour's Lost
Hamlet

RADIO

1993
The Monday Play – BBC Radio 4
The Strange Case of Dr Jekyll and Mr Hyde – BBC Radio 4

1996
Paint Her Well – BBC Radio 4

1998
The Airmen Who Would Not Die – BBC Radio 4

2000

The Sunday Play – BBC Radio 3

2001

Dr Finlay: Adventures of A Black Bag – BBC Radio 4

Much Ado About Nothing – BBC Radio 3

2002

Double Income, No Kids Yet – BBC Radio 4

Flames: Physics – BBC Radio 4

Island – BBC Radio 4

The Museum – BBC Radio 4

2003

A Quick Change – BBC Radio 4

Caesar – BBC Radio 4

Double Income No Kids Yet – BBC Radio 4

Strangers and Brothers – BBC Radio 4

The Rotter's Club – BBC Radio 4

Tuesdays and Sundays – BBC Radio 4

2005

Dixon Of Dock Green – BBC Radio 4

2006

The Feast of the Drowned – by Stephen Cole

The Resurrection Casket – by Justin Richards

The Stone Rose — by Jacqueline Rayner
Virgin Panto — Virgin Radio

2007
Doctor Who Audio Books
The Wooden Overcoat — BBC Radio 4

MISCELLANEOUS AUDIO BOOKS

1998
Macbeth — by William Shakespeare
Romeo and Juliet — by William Shakespeare

1999
Comedy of Errors — by William Shakespeare
Much Ado About Nothing — by William Shakespeare

2000
King Henry VI — by William Shakespeare
The Merlin Conspiracy — by Diana Wynne Jones

2004
How to be a Pirate — by Cressida Cowell
How to Train your Dragon — by Cressida Cowell
King Lear — by William Shakespeare
Quite Ugly One Morning — by Christopher Brookmyre

A LIFE IN TIME AND SPACE

Starter for Ten – by David Nicholls

The Merchant of Venice – by William Shakespeare

Whiteout – by Ken Follett

2005

Hairy Maclary From Donaldson's Dairy – by Lynley Dodd

The Beasts of Clawstone Castle – by Eva Ibbotson

2006

Hairy Maclary's Rumpus At The Vet – by Lynley Dodd

How to Speak Dragonese – by Cressida Cowell

2007

Hairy Maclary's Bone – by Lynley Dodd

How to Cheat a Dragon's Curse – by Cressida Cowell

DAVID TENNANT'S DOCTOR WHO EPISODE GUIDE 2005–2008

This listing relates only to the episodes and Christmas specials in which David Tennant has appeared. The data was complied from information logged at the British Film Institute Library in London, from the Internet Movie Database (imdb.com) and from Wikipedia (wikipedia.org).

Series 1, Episode 13: 'The Parting of the Ways'.

Written by Russell T. Davies. Directed by Joe Ahearne.
Aired: 18 June 2005.

Christmas Special: 'The Christmas Invasion'

Written by Russell T. Davies. Directed by James Hawes
Aired: 25 December 2005.

Series 2, Episode 1: 'New Earth'

Written by Russell T. Davies. Directed by James Hawes.
Aired: 15 April 2006.

Series 2, Episode 2: 'Tooth and Claw'

Written by Russell T. Davies. Directed by Euros Lyn.
Aired: 22 April 2006.

Series 2, Episode 3: 'School Reunion'

Written by Toby Whitehouse. Directed by James Hawes.
Aired: 29 April 2006.

Series 2, Episode 4: 'The Girl in the Fireplace'

Written by Steven Moffat. Directed by Euros Lyn.
Aired: 6 May 2006.

Series 2, Episode 5: 'Rise of the Cyberman'

Written by Tom Macrae. Directed by Graeme Harper.
Aired: 13 May 2006.

Series 2, Episode 6: 'The Age of Steel'

Written by Tom Macrae. Directed by Graeme Harper.
Aired: 20 May 2006.

Series 2, Episode 7: 'The Idiot's Lantern'

Written by Mark Gattis. Directed by Euros Lyn.
Aired: 27 May 2006.

Series 2, Episode 8: 'The Impossible Planet'

Written by Matt Jones. Directed by James Strong.

Aired: 3 June 2006.

Series 2, Episode 9: 'The Satan Pit'

Written by Matt Jones. Directed by James Strong.

Aired: 10 June 2006.

Series 2, Episode 10: 'Love and Monsters'

Written by Russell T. Davies. Directed by Dan Zeff.

Aired: 17 June 2006.

Series 2, Episode 11: 'Fear Her'

Written by Matthew Graham. Directed by Euros Lyn.

Aired: 24 June 2006.

Series 2, Episode 12: 'Army of Ghosts'

Written by Russell T. Davies. Directed by Graeme Harper.

Aired: 1 July 2006.

Series 2, Episode 13: 'Doomsday'

Written by Russell T. Davies. Directed by Graeme Harper.

Aired: 8 July 2006.

Christmas Special: 'The Runaway Bride'

Written by Russell T. Davies. Directed by Euros Lynn.

Aired: 25 December 2006.

Series 3, Episode 1: 'Smith and Jones'

Written by Russell T. Davies. Directed by Charles Palmer.
Aired: 31 March 2007.

Series 3, Episode 2: 'The Shakespeare Code'

Written by Gareth Roberts. Directed by Charles Palmer.
Aired: 7 April 2007.

Series 3, Episode 3: 'Gridlock'

Written by Russell T. Davies. Directed by Richard Clark.
Aired: 14 April 2007.

Series 3, Episode 4: 'Daleks in Manhattan'

Written by Helen Raynor. Directed by James Strong.
Aired: 21 April 2007.

Series 3, Episode 5: 'Evolution of the Daleks'

Written by Helen Raynor. Directed by James Strong.
Aired: 28 April 2007.

Series 3, Episode 6: 'The Lazarus Experiment'

Written by Stephen Greenhorn. Directed by Richard Clark.
Aired: 5 May 2007.

Series 3, Episode 7: '42'

Written by Chris Chibnall. Directed by Graeme Harper.
Aired: 19 May 2007.

Series 3, Episode 8: 'Human Nature'

Written by Paul Cornell. Directed by Charles Palmer.

Aired: 26 May 2007.

Series 3, Episode 9: 'The Family of Blood'

Written by Paul Cornell. Directed by Charles Palmer.

Aired: 2 June 2007.

Series 3, Episode 10: 'Blink'

Written by Steven Moffat. Directed by Hettie MacDonald.

Aired: 9 June 2007.

Series 3, Episode 11: 'Utopia'

Written by Russell T. Davies. Directed by Graeme Harper.

Aired: 16 June 2007.

Series 3, Episode 12: 'The Sound of Drums'

Written by Russell T. Davies. Directed by Colin Teague.

Aired: 23 June 2007.

Series 3, Episode 13: 'Last of the Time Lords'

Written by Russell T. Davies. Directed by Colin Teague.

Aired: 30 June 2007.

Christmas Special: 'Voyage of the Damned'

Written by Russell T. Davies. Directed by James Strong.

Aired: 25 December 2007.

Series 4, Episode 1: 'Partners in Crime'

Written by Russell T. Davies. Directed by James Strong.
Aired: 5 April 2008.

Series 4, Episode 2: 'The Fires of Pompeii'

Written by James Moran. Directed by Colin Teague.
Aired: 12 April 2008.

Series 4, Episode 3: 'Planet of Ood'

Written by Keith Temple. Directed by Graeme Harper.
Aired: 19 April 2008.

Series 4, Episode 4: 'The Sontaran Stratagem'

Written by Helen Raynor. Directed by Douglas Mackinnon.
Aired: 26 April 2008.

Series 4, Episode 5: 'The Poison Sky'

Written by Helen Raynor. Directed by Douglas Mackinnon. Aired:
3 May 2008.

Series 4, Episode 6: 'The Doctor's Daughter'

Written by Stephen Greenhorn. Directed by Alice Troughton.
Aired: 10 May 2008.

Series 4, Episode 7: 'The Unicorn and the Wasp'

Written by Gareth Roberts. Directed by Graeme Harper.
Aired: 17 May 2008.

Series 4, Episode 8: 'Silence in the Library'

Written by Steven Moffat. Directed by Euros Lyn.

Aired: 31 May 2008.

Series 4, Episode 9: 'Forest of the Dead'

Written by Steven Moffat. Directed by Euros Lyn.

Aired: 7 June 2008.

Series 4, Episode 10: 'Midnight'

Written by Russell T. Davis. Directed by Alice Troughton.

Aired: 14 June 2008.

Series 4, Episode 11: 'Turn Left'

Written by Russell T. Davies, Directed by Graeme Harper.

Aired: 21 June 2008.

Series 4, Episode 12: 'The Stolen Earth'

Written by Russell T. Davies. Directed by Graeme Harper.

Aired: 28 June 2008.

Series 4, Episode 13: 'Journey's End'

Written by Russell T. Davies. Directed by Graeme Harper.

Aired: 5 July 2008.

AWARDS AND
NOMINATIONS

AWARDS

2005

- Critics Award for Theatre in Scotland – Best Male for Jimmy Porter in *Look Back in Anger*

2006

- *Doctor Who Magazine* Readers Survey – Best Actor To Play the Doctor
- *Heat* magazine Reader Survey – Best TV Acting Performance
- Pink Paper Awards – The Sexiest Man In The Universe
- *Radio Times* Review of the Year – Hero of The Year
- *Radio Times* Review of the Year – TV Moment of the Year (*Doctor Who*: 'Doomsday' Finale)
- The National Television Awards – Most Popular Actor

- The National Television Awards – Most Popular Drama for *Doctor Who*
- The Scottish Style Awards – Most Stylish Male
- TV Quick & TV Choice Awards – Best Actor
- *TV Times* Readers Awards – Favourite Actor
- *TV Times* Readers' Awards – Favourite TV Show (*Doctor Who*)

2007

- BAFTA Cymru Awards – Best Actor
- BBC Drama Awards – Best Actor
- BBC Drama Awards – Best Drama (*Doctor Who*)
- BBC Drama Awards, Best Drama Website – BBC *Doctor Who* site; also placed 'David-Tennant.com'
- BBC Drama Awards – Favourite Moment (*Doctor Who*: Rose's Exit'); also placed for 'The Daleks Vs The Cybermen'
- Glenfiddich Spirit of Scotland Awards – Screen Star
- *Heat* magazine Reader Survey – Best Acting Performance
- Scotland on Sunday Greatest Ever Scots – Best Actor
- Scotland on Sunday's Most Eligible Male Poll – 1st Place
- Scots Care Comedy Awards: Scotland's Greatest Comedy Moment – for Catherine Tate Comic Relief Sketch
- SFX Sci Fi Awards – Sexiest Male
- The National Television Awards – Most Popular Actor
- The National Television Awards – Most Popular Drama for *Doctor Who*
- *TV Quick* & *TV Choice* Awards – Best Actor
- UKTV Drama *Doctor Who* Award – Best Doctor Ever

NOMINATIONS

2000

- Ian Charleson Award – Best Classical Actor Under 30 for *Comedy of Errors*

2003

- Olivier Award – Best Actor (as Jeff in *Lobby Hero*)

2005

- The Scottish Style Awards – Most Stylish Male

2007

- *Hello!* magazine poll – Most Attractive Male of 2007
- Nickelodeon Kids TV Awards – Best Television Actor
- The Scottish Style Awards – Most Stylish Male

The following books by Nigel Goodall can now be purchased from your local bookshop or direct from his publisher:

Fearne Cotton — The Biography
ISBN 978 1 84454 584 1
HB £17.99

The Secret World of Johnny Depp
ISBN 978 1 84454 387 8
PB £7.99

Being Davina
ISBN 978 1 84454 385 4
PB £7.99

Christian Slater — The Biography
ISBN 978 1 84454 137 9
HB £17.99

Free P+P and UK Delivery
(Abroad £3.00 per book)

TO ORDER SIMPLY CALL THIS NUMBER:
+ 44 (0) 207 381 0666

Or visit our website www.blake.co.uk

Prices and availability subject to change without notice

RAY WINSTONE
– THE BIOGRAPHY

Nigel Goodall

From the rough streets of the East End to the red carpets of glitzy award shows, Ray Winstone has seen it all. And, notching up more than 100 appearances on screen over the years, he is now regarded as one of the foremost actors of his generation and the ultimate screen hard man.

He is more than just another on-screen tough guy; he portrays violence as it really is. Coming from humble beginnings, he has learnt first hand how tough life can be. Every inch the rebel in his youth, he was expelled from drama school less than a year after deciding to pursue his dream. But Ray didn't let this put him off … And it was this, his cocky aggressive attitude, that led director Alan Clarke to believe he would be so perfect for the lead role in Scum. And he hasn't looked back since!

Over the years, working with some of the finest directors in the business, Ray has achieved success on the stage, as well as on both the small- and the big-screen.

In this, the first ever biography of the unflinching star, prize-nominated author Nigel Goodall provides a fascinating insight into the intriguing life of the rebel made good. Painstakingly researched, and drenched in Ray's own gritty dialogue, for once we get to see the man behind the tough guy exterior.

ISBN 978 1 84454 659 6

John Blake Publishing Ltd

COMING IN PAPERBACK SOON